# THE ULTIMATE OVERSEAS BUSINESS GUIDE FOR GROWING COMPANIES

# THE ULTIMATE OVERSEAS BUSINESS GUIDE FOR GROWING COMPANIES

*Henry H. Rodkin*

**Dow Jones-Irwin**
Homewood, Illinois 60430

Sponsoring editor: Susan Glinert Stevens, Ph.D.
Project editor: Lynne Basler
Production manager: Ann Cassady
Cover design: Michael S. Finkelman
Compositor: Eastern Graphics
Typeface: 11/13 Century Schoolbook
Printer: Arcata Graphics/Kingsport

**Library of Congress Cataloging-in-Publication Data**

Rodkin, Henry H.
The ultimate overseas business guide for growing companies / Henry H. Rodkin.
p. cm.
ISBN 1-55623-300-0
1. Corporations, American—European Economic Community countries—Management. 2. Corporations, American—Management. 3. Export marketing. I. Title.
HD70.E86R64 1990
658.8′48—dc20 89–29372
CIP

*Printed in the United States of America*
1 2 3 4 5 6 7 8 9 0 K 7 6 5 4 3 2 1 0

*This book is dedicated*
*to three special people in my life:*
*Maggie, Nancy, and Jill, my wife and daughters,*
*who encouraged and coerced me into doing this.*

*This book is also written to honor four people*
*who influenced my life and the way I think:*
*Sadie Friedlander, history teacher,*
*Hyde Park High School, Chicago, 1951, 1952*
*Herbert Prescott, English teacher, Grinnell College, 1953, 1954*
*Jack Sissors, journalism teacher, Northwestern University, 1955, 1956*
*Pierre Martineau, behavioral scientist,* The Chicago Tribune, *1963, 1964*

# INTRODUCTION

When the U.S. dollar weakens, as it has in the recent past in terms of its value against other currencies of the world, there is virtually no excuse for American business not to be exporting more of its output. When the value of the dollar drops against the yen or the deutsch mark or the pound or the franc, our goods and services cost less in Japan, Germany, Great Britain, and France, and their output costs more here. While all of this works in our favor, our overseas price advantage in some cases sadly even supersedes deficiencies in quality and production of American goods sent abroad. . . . My friends and former business colleagues in Sweden, Finland, Germany, Australia, and Japan have told me repeatedly of production delays and quality issues they have encountered with some of their imported U.S. goods, but they have always added that the current low price of American goods, because of the weak dollar, more often than not had offset those issues of normal concern to any buyer. Their business in selling U.S. products grows every year, in part because they enjoy a price advantage against locally manufactured items whenever the exchange rate causes the dollar to slip. If we can establish markets and develop a franchise abroad despite quality problems, imagine what the future might offer with products engineered and made well! Yet, the United States continues to show huge trade imbalances that are absolutely inexcusable, given the desires of world buyers for American goods and services, an extension of the world's basic desire to emulate a great many things "American."

If you believe in the strength and the ingenuity of American industry, and believe that most domestic manufacturers are indeed making great strides in production quality, then there may *never* really be a bad time to be an exporter, cheap dollar or not; the notion of establishing a business and building a franchise in other markets *now* can sustain a business in the future regardless of the strength or weakness of the dollar, but you have to recognize what your strengths might be versus the competition overseas, competition from other U.S. companies as well as significant foreign competition.

In the next few years, the European Economic Community (EEC) will eliminate any current intercountry trade barriers; they talk of a common trade currency. In this country, people talk about the EEC as a potential "United States of Europe," and they think the economic strength of that union abroad will just be another slice out of our economic well-being, but how many of these economic prophets have been involved in any business dealings with Europeans where their American-made products offered something special and unique to the buyer? Have they ever spent much time socially with their European business counterparts or their customers? Have they ever conducted any real market research efforts in European trade to learn and understand the levels of buyer awareness or the sense of perceived value of products made in the United States of America versus other countries? Most of all, have they ever taken the time to create the genuine relationships that are so important and so often seem to transcend even legal contracts in the conduct of business with people in another culture? These are all opportunities to learn and to understand how we can be successful in developing business beyond these shores.

In 1997, Hong Kong will become part of the People's Republic of China (PRC). Hong Kong operates on a U.S. dollar standard which makes it quite unique in the Asian marketplace, a very powerful enclave of business where values are pegged to a currency we can understand—ours! But how many businesses operate in the United States with any consideration of Hong Kong and the possible impact of what will happen in 1997, or the Asian market in general, other than Japan.

I remember in 1985 visiting with associates in Hong Kong, who were desperately trying to convince their 20- and 30-year-old children to emigrate to Australia rather than relive their parents' experiences, which caused them to flee the mainland in 1949. But the PRC is different from what it was 40 years ago, and events right now in China, with millions of people marching for democracy in Beijing, I hope, may never allow it to return to its conservatism of the past. The emotional energy being expended by older businesspeople in Hong Kong, based on their experiences of a few decades ago, may not be totally reasoned, but whoever said reason should prevail at all times? Yet this too may be an opportunity to find distribution options, manufacturing advantages, and trading partners in a bountiful area of the world.

About a century ago, Great Britain was the dominant country in world trade. The United States, perhaps grudgingly, emerged after World War II as the dominant industrial power, and Japan crept up on us in the 1960s to reach a point of extraordinary strength today. Korea might very well be the next explosive growth factor in international economics, followed perhaps by Brazil or Thailand.

If we take the time to look at the factors that make these changes occur, and if we attempt to maintain a base of knowledge and experience in these emerging cultures, we can share in the opportunities available with this continued development and growth all over the world.

The point is clear: there are ways to do business abroad based on opportunities that will exist because someone has overreacted, because someone has never reacted, or because someone has used good sense, but you have to try. The old axiom, "nothing ventured, nothing gained," will always hold true.

When I began to think the contents of this book might be worth sharing with others, I was convinced these experiences and anecdotes would be for medium-sized and small companies who were not well-developed sophisticates of international business, companies who might somehow dabble in overseas trade or work with export management companies or wish to do something overseas but lack what they felt was the experience-base to embark on such a business-building venture.

Reflecting further on that opinion, and having now found the time to read and hear more about corporate wins and losses overseas, I am more convinced than ever that only a handful of

U.S. companies have ever really taken the time "to do it well." My former employer, Procter & Gamble, entered Japan in 1972 to gain a major foothold in the disposable diaper business and with household detergents. By the mid-1980s, P&G had losses in Japan in excess of $200 million! I considered Procter & Gamble to be my advanced degree course in marketing after I'd worked there. Learning how to be competitive and responsive in a marketplace was the Procter way, but it took them a great many years and dollars to learn the hard way how to be effective in markets like Japan. While they currently enjoy a greater than 20 percent share of the disposable diaper market in Japan, why didn't their people understand cultural differences and what the Japanese people wanted sooner? Conversely, they should be commended for their ability and desire to stay until the market was understood.

In 1974, about halfway through my business career, I was instructed to make something out of my then-current employer's export business and their overseas factory locations. The company had indeed turned itself around in the U.S. market for automotive replacement products, and international markets seemed a logical next step. Our U.S. business had grown with revamped, exciting products, contemporary advertising and promotion, and an extraordinary distribution system that guaranteed very high order-fill rates within 24 hours. The extent of my "experience" in anything overseas was high school and college German 20 years before, two vacation trips to Europe, and a trip once to Puerto Rico! Our U.S. product line was limited to replacement parts for European and Japanese cars sold in this country. The "significant" markets were Puerto Rico, the Philippines, and a few areas in Latin America, with a total sales volume of about $2.5 million.

Within five years, our export sales had increased to over $30 million, and we had become the leading brand in several European markets. We were challenging market leaders in several other large markets, and we were clearly "on a roll." We established a brand franchise of such real value that when we asked a distributor if he would take a private-label product at a discounted price, he paled and pleaded that we shouldn't joke around.

All of this was done with a staff that, although quite small, had a great deal of dedication and concern and a solid focus on product quality and availability of items requested and needed by the markets into which they were sold. Our customers knew they could send us new product introductions from competitors, and that we would fill out our/their line with great speed to enable them to remain competitive.

The chapters in this book began as speech topics used in various places: a training conference for export service people, the marketing clubs of the graduate business schools at the University of Chicago and Northwestern University, an Advertising Age workshop, "Not Invented Here," and an International Advertising Association luncheon. The stories were based on varied experiences in Europe, the Far East, the Middle East, Australia/New Zealand, South America, and Mexico, and they came from my travels as vice president, marketing, in the international operations of an automotive parts manufacturer and as president of international operations for a Fortune 500 conglomerate in leisure and industrial products.

In their enlarged versions for this book, the elements of these stories remain the same: overseas customers expect certain things from us as Americans. In general, they have a very fixed notion of us and of this country. You will certainly succeed by developing a sensitivity to these people overseas and the cultures in which they live, and you will certainly succeed when you combine that sensitivity with remaining what you are, an American. This is an opportunity of nearly limitless proportion, but you have to be innovative, creative, and above all, understanding of your new customers.

You will never be a success as a "cultural chameleon." Don't try to be what your customers are, or forget to be what you are. You cannot be a Japanese or a Chinese, no matter how much you learn about them; you cannot be an Arab or a Swede or a German or a Frenchman. The attributes these and other people will look for in you have probably been gleaned from TV, movies, and any other source of mass communication about the United States. This is, in part, what they will expect from you. This book will discuss this issue as well as many others in helping you toward whatever goal you set to increase your business in overseas markets.

I have included various outlines, tables, and charts in this book. Even while some statistics are helpful in making a point clear or in determining a direction to take, I believe that the understanding of more subtle influences in relationships in doing business with others abroad can be of significantly greater value in the long run. There is a warmer side of doing business, a side that is fun; it can be rewarding, and can surely help everyone in mutual understanding, more business, and profitability.

**Henry H. Rodkin**

# CONTENTS

# CHAPTER 1

# ALL IS NOT PRICE

## or "QUALITY, SERVICE, AND UNIQUENESS STILL COUNT"

Quite often, the attitude of people considering doing business abroad seems to be that the only way to compete with "those people" is to beat "their" price in the marketplace, or, if all else fails, to match their price and then try something mystically defined as "outmarketing them." Too often we hear that a company wants to be "marketing driven," but the author of that comment generally doesn't really know what marketing is.

When all knowledge and insight fail, the answer does not have to be price alone, especially when this argument too often becomes merely a rationalization for the alternative of doing nothing: "How can we compete with those guys; they are subsidized by their government, and we can't match their prices." Even being marketing driven won't help management with that attitude.

### PROTECTIONISM IS A TWO-WAY STREET

Trade barriers are also used as an excuse to rationalize a decision to do nothing. If you are in the paperboard business, you know that the Japanese require board of a smoothness not often made in this country. American hogs aren't generally exported into Canada because there is a 30-day Canadian quarantine period, and U.S. farmers don't want to hold the livestock. U.S. patents and trademarks are extremely vulnerable on electronics going into Brazil or Taiwan and on pharmaceuticals that might go into Argentina, Mexico, South Korea, or Taiwan.

Try being an Argentinian or Australian meat producer, however, with thoughts of exporting to this country. Our import levels vary with the slaughter rates on U.S. cattle. That may sound fair to us, just as an Indian textile worker may feel protected by his country's ban on textile and clothing imports.

Sugar imports into the United States are limited to 2.5 million short tons, and carbon steel imports are limited to one-fifth of the market. Everyone, it seems, plays the game on everyone else, and those who want the most protection seem to complain the most about why and how they cannot develop an overseas business presence.

## LOW-COST PRODUCTION IS A WEAK RESPONSE

When markets are open and trade is basically "free," the U.S. management response may be one of trying to be the low-cost producer in order to succeed abroad, but, too often, low cost implies removing the factors that allow one product to be differentiated from another. Competitive efforts become blunted, and selling success becomes dependent on the commodity now being sold, not the product.

Additionally, low cost tends to establish a situation where there are simply insufficient funds to support any sales promotion and advertising efforts on behalf of a product. Market entry then becomes an impossibility, and the management response is to look for government protection, subsidies, and the like.

If exporting is loaded with so many obstacles, or if firms strategize to export in less than positive ways through quality cutting, or if management rationalizes itself into oblivion, how can we explain the following successes in that nemesis market Japan:

- McDonald's controls 30 percent of the fast-food hamburger market.

- Braun shavers, owned by Gillette, own 40 percent of that market.
- Kodak has 12–15 percent of the amateur film market.

*The Wall Street Journal*, April 16, 1989.

There are generally tangible reasons why an American product should be purchased overseas if it enjoys any degree of success in the United States. This society is so heterogeneous that you can be sure there is some segment of the U.S. market for your product, and this segment is probably representative, as well, of some of the tastes of a foreign market you want to enter. In any event, quite often the perceived glamour of an American item will help if all else fails. If not, why should Kodak be able to compete in Japan with Fuji? How can Schick have 70 percent of the safety razor blade market in Japan?

## PRODUCT DIFFERENTIATION: THE REAL KEY TO SUCCESS

If and when you make the decision to sell overseas, think about those things in your product that differentiate it from others, not only features engineered into the product, but also elements of customer service, distribution, or even invoicing that might give you an edge against someone else. A simple technique is to array your product virtues on a list alongside all you know about your competitor's products. Even if you think your final price is high, margin for a distributor, commissions for a sales representative, and product performance for the buyer should always be dominant in a truly competitive war, here or overseas.

If there is nothing left for you after you play this game solely on price to be competitive, where is the advantage in trying at all?

## LEARN THE MARKET'S SECRETS

If you don't know much about your competition, be absolutely sure to learn before you elect to wage a market war against them. While this subject is covered in greater detail in Chapter 12 on market intelligence, "Overseas Research, Intelligence, and NIH," the following stories may illustrate this point and set the stage for other chapters. They are mentioned here, however, because they serve to show that knowing what is in a market, recognizing what buyers want, and responding to those needs will always prevail over simply offering a low price.

## Mexico: A Problem in Distribution

In the early 1980s the time came to be serious about an operation my firm had in Mexico. The management of that company continued to feel they were the market leader although unit and dollar (or peso) sales and profit were declining year after year.

When asked how a market leader could watch this year-after-year decline, the answer was that the Mexican economy was in a long, slow decline (it was), and that people simply were not buying. While this was one of the classic rationales not to act, but rather to save what is already there (at least for the short run), it was hard to accept when published financial data indicated that the only substantive competitor in the marketplace was growing enough to warrant and finance a new factory!

It was indeed time to look into the market at both selling and buying levels to see what was happening, and we needed to know why the brand was in decline. As outsiders from the United States, we felt that a college professor in Mexico City would be the resource to help provide the answers. A meeting was established with our management in Mexico, and the professor helped to set up a research plan to determine three basic things:

1. The scope of distribution for the overall product category in which we operated, that is, what could we learn about our wholesalers and those of the competition?
2. The magnitude of the competition's presence within the distribution system, that is, where was their strength?
3. The feelings and attitudes of customers within the prod-

uct category, the competition's and ours, in terms of what made people buy, that is, why did anyone buy anyone's product?

Lest anyone think this is something only major corporations can do, the total cost of this project was $5,000. Within 30 days we were together, reviewing the findings.

The research categorized distribution by size of outlet, from A, large, to C, small. We learned there was a relatively new entry in the distribution system, selling directly to the ultimate consumer at the same retail price as the traditional distribution system, which had an extra step; the new entry into distribution was making a wonderful profit by eliminating one step in the sales process, and they were rapidly gaining market share—at our expense!

As expected, and now proved, we were weak with the A-level distributors, we had modest strength with B and C, but the new direct sale outlets were stealing business from everyone, and they were exclusively selling the competition product. An exciting new source of sales had developed in the marketplace, and our management had not been given enough information from the field to know about it in any great detail.

This preliminary information, in addition to telling us about the scope of this new sales avenue, also told us we might be able to sell a new entry product at a higher price, but we needed to know more. At this point, we actually had the beginnings of two strategies: first, we were being shown an area where we had not developed any business, and second, the research gave us information on what people sought to make a buying decision about our products.

By using the customer and distributor comments to actually sell the product which we obtained in the research, we felt we could stop the erosion of the brand's franchise in its current distribution setup and perhaps even build it back up if we initiated a good advertising campaign directed to the customer base buying within that distribution.

We contacted the Mexico City office of a U.S. advertising agency (U.S. agency offices are all over the world, as further evidence that the United States knows how to advertise/promote probably better than anyone!), and began the development of an advertising campaign using newspapers, outdoor advertising, and radio. Working together with the staff of that office, who really understood the subtleties of the market, we were able to tell the buyer audience basically what they wanted to know about the product. After all, the research had told us! Slowly but surely, we began to rebuild the distribution and sale of the product within the A, B, and C channels of distribution.

Curiously, this strategy led the competitor to believe we had ignored their new sales channel. They thought we were simply working to maintain the traditional part of the business, while they were being allowed to go merrily along in their own area of sales success.

While our campaign was under way, however, we began a second market research study into that new channel of distribution. Why only eat one course in this restaurant when the whole menu might be available with a little more effort?

The new research was designed to find out if the new channel might accept a special, unique-to-itself brand: its own private label. The competitor was selling the same product there as they were in their A through C outlets. Further, pricing was also becoming an issue that mitigated against their strength in both; that is, the competition was selling in at the same price even though the new distribution system was selling directly to the end buyer and the traditional system had another step. As a result, pricing on the competitive brand was a bit haywire in the marketplace, and buyers were becoming sensitive to it, seeking bargain pricing at any and all sales outlets.

We wanted to see if we could enter the new distribution channel in a more orderly fashion with a special private label at a special (higher) price. This sector would now have its own product and a shortened distribution system that would allow for higher selling-in prices, yet lower retail prices. (With one less element in the system, there was one less margin to cover!)

The original brand was growing again, and it was easier to consider financing another research study. The results indicated that a private-label line identifiable only within this new channel would not only be accepted but was hoped for by the businesses within it. Further, they were willing to pay a 10 percent premium for their own private-label product, and we knew we were going to win.

The product name we tested was well accepted, and we now had to be careful that we followed through correctly on every aspect of what would become a new business area for us, and, we hoped, a loss for the competitor. We changed the cosmetic appearance of the most successful item in the existing line, repainting it on the line and reboxing it for shipment to this end of the business.

We began informal meetings with the people pegged to be our new customers, and the research was further validated by their overwhelmingly favorable responses. There was no reason to charge a low price to enter this new market and to be an effective player in that sales contest.

## Local Markets, Different Responses

One of the extra things learned in this Mexican endeavor was that Latin American buyers often tend to equate low price with low quality, and that catering to their real needs as consumers, in much the same fashion as we would to any major buying segment in this country, would yield far better results with better profits for everyone involved.

The Mexican company's fortunes were once again on the rise. We had caught the competition totally off guard and had taken away a major segment of their business with a product giving us a greater profit. Further, we had strengthened ourselves in the more traditional area of distribution, shutting them off from growth there. There were no four for three sales, no initial selling-in discounts, and all was not price.

Another market presented a totally different problem, however.

## A Look at German Differences

We were latecomers in Germany in a field crowded with product made all over Europe and the United States. The distribution network appeared to be crowded and monopolized by local manufacturers vying with each other for market share. In this market where taxis are often Mercedes Benz automobiles, it was highly questionable if price would be an effective tool for market entry!

In spite of the obvious, we charged into the market with better pricing and a German sales manager recruited from the competition. After a few years of trying, and after no profits and very limited distribution around the country, it was obvious that we had to do something different. Price didn't seem to be the answer, but we weren't sure of that yet and we didn't know what was.

We decided to examine what distributor and dealer perceptions were for our product and all others in five major cities; then we hoped we would be able to reestablish a proper strategy while we were hanging on by our proverbial fingertips. The research was initiated after weeks of reviewing questionnaires to determine that we were indeed seeking viable data, and we waited to see the results with great anxiety. When the information came back, we synthesized it into a marketing strategy and went to see the German sales manager.

Before we could even begin to discuss the research and our new plans, he announced that his field salesmen had surveyed the market to complement our work and that he already knew what the problems were. In summary, he felt we were "too pricey." He had learned that the British had entered the market with a product line offering deeper discounts and, of course, even lower prices than ours. He concluded by announcing we would have to suffer yet another round of price reductions and absent profits to fight off the British in this market if we expected to achieve any long-term success in Germany.

Fortunately, we had prepared the research quite well. We knew what we had to learn, and we recognized what we would have to do as soon as the information came back. Independent field survey teams, not representing themselves as our employees, had questioned the trade at all levels to determine awareness of our product versus others and to pinpoint the various strengths and weaknesses of every product in the market, ours included.

## Buyer Perceptions Are Vital

The issue in the marketplace was not price, but perception and our performance in distribution. American manufacturers in many areas of business had turned away from developing any real business in Germany; they were looked at as not being serious about the market, and this perception was often intensified by a U.S. company's manufacturing decision not to build in deep engineering qualities generally expected by the Germans. As for the British product, in spite of our sales manager's urging that we reduce prices further to compete with that product, the German trade had indicated in our research that they would never buy a product made in Britain, regardless of price.

Our research about this German perception of British merchandise was valid; we saved a great deal of money and a lot of reputation by not lowering our price to compete with a product that was withdrawn from the market a short while later. For our product, we embarked on a long-range plan to enhance our image and our presence. Clearly, we had to create awareness in buyers about our long history as a company, our built-in quality, our inventories in the market and consequent availability on a level with locally made product, and, most important, our desire to stay in the market.

Halfway around the world, we were to address yet another problem where we thought price was the answer.

## Japan: 1,000 Different Correct Answers

A frightening example of overreacting on price happened in Japan, and in many respects, Japan is probably where most people can expect to have very different and unique sets of problems.

Relationships are vital in Japan, and unlike a great many places in this world, they won't develop overnight. When I arrived in Japan for the first time, I was met at the airport by our distributor's representative who whisked me into Tokyo in a company car, registered with me at the hotel, and immediately asked where I wanted to have dinner. Jet lag aside, this was going to be a test of anyone's fortitude!

The next day we visited various sights of interest and culture, and on the third day we took the bullet train to Osaka where the distributor's headquarters were located, and where we would begin to discuss the product line his company had seemingly agreed to carry on our behalf. You should note that this was the first time in 40 years that we had a chance to have our product in distribution, available for sale in Japan. Prior to World War II, our product had enjoyed great success in that market; now, 30 years after the war, we were trying again.

Without my knowing it, our distributor was attempting to establish the rudiments of a relationship by escorting me into his culture prior to our business meetings; at this point, early in my career in international business, I had not yet taken the time to learn very much about Japan except that the word *shrimp* was *ebi* and some other basic phrases.

## Price As a Misperceived Market Entry Tool

With this prelude, let us continue the saga of selling in Japan and the issue of price. My management had been convinced that a low, low price was needed to reinstate ourselves in this market against the major local manufacturers. To further enhance this flawed belief, I was told that the place to start was by having Tokyo taxis endorse the product (shock absorbers) by having them installed during service cycles. This "professional endorsement" was to be the key to our return!

By not recognizing that the Japanese require a great amount of etiquette and form to precede and even engulf their dealings, we had begun a relationship that would be loaded with errors, misunderstandings, and sad results. In effect, we went into the market believing that all we needed was low price.

Japanese form has created a very rigid code of behavior, with accompanying embarrasssments and misdirections if the form is not maintained. While things are not as rigid and unforgiving as they were in the times of the samurai, the Japanese business world has certain expectations about how people should act, react, and interact. This was to play an important role in that first visit to Japan.

## The Elements of Japanese Form versus a Crazy American

Harmony on the surface must be sustained always. Regardless of what you are thinking, you must maintain an even attitude with your associates. Harmony can even be of greater value than truth if truth will be disruptive to the group. As an extension of this attitude on harmony, confrontation is truly very bad form.

Walking down the street with a Japanese one time, I asked if another person would become angry and confrontational if he or she were tripped by someone. The answer: "No one would trip someone else in Japan." That comment was the essence of what we should have known early in the game, but didn't until much later.

Imagine the tragedy of what now follows. After several days of meetings and discussions, we finally sat down to discuss the product line and PRICE. Being a classic American marketing type with a solid training base from Procter & Gamble, I was prepared to convince my Japanese counterparts they were in error in asking for the low prices they wanted. Not only was I going to show them the error of their ways, but in typical American fashion I was going to be a bit confrontational as well. So much for form and harmony!

U.S. embassy personnel had checked pricing for me, obtaining levels for every distribution segment of the market; my manager, in his eagerness to succeed in Japan, had preceded me and had offered prices substantially below where we had to be; my embassy-produced information verified that. Unfortunately, that data would ultimately destroy the harmony we had been building up prior to sitting down for a price meeting in Osaka.

The only information that should have been used was that potential buyers perceived our product as having less quality than others because of the low, low prices, but that point was not to emerge in the meetings we had in those early days in Japan for our company.

## Epilogue on a Japanese Experience

Fortunately, I spent many more years traveling to Japan on business after that first visit in 1975. The original distributor was less scrupulous than one would expect in Japan, and we caught him violating his distribution contract, transshipping goods across the Soviet Union for resale in Finland.

With a new distributor and more experience on my part, we developed a warm and lasting friendship with a Japanese business associate who taught me about *wa* and *shibumi* as concepts of group and individual harmony, as well as showing me the subtle elements in the language and in life in Japan.

We concentrated our selling efforts into market niches in Japan that were untapped by the local manufacturers—niches where buyers wanted to identify with certain American styles and mannerisms. Our margins were high, and those of our distributor and his customers were equally strong, but more important, consumer needs were being met by their perceptions of the performance of our product. We had a franchise of lasting value in a market where the local competitors even tried to legislate our exclusion to no avail!

## SUMMARY

Whenever you face the decision of whether or not you wish to expand your business by exploiting overseas markets, remember to consider whether or not you have a product of real value with discernible differences for the buyer.

Be sure you take enough time to learn about the market in terms of distribution systems, personalities of the people with whom you will be working, and what the trends may be for your product, your product category, and buyer tastes and needs.

Do not ever simply transfer promotional techniques to another market without first understanding the role played in that market by price. Remember to understand the need for research and knowledge, and that seeking the answers is possible only when you know what the questions are.

# APPENDIX

## UNITED STATES IMPORT QUOTAS

As discussed in this chapter, import restrictions and quotas are a two-way street. As you consider exporting, the opportunity to import will also become quite obvious. You should, therefore, know what the restrictions are before a seeming opportunity vanishes in the face of our law.

An import quota is a quantity control on certain goods for a certain period of time. All quotas are developed through legislation and proclamations of the President. Quotas can be *absolute* or *tariff rate.*

Absolute quotas will limit the quantity of goods in a category that may be brought into this country in a specified period of time. When the absolute quota is filled, no further importation is allowed during the import period; this has been the case, in the past, with certain size Japanese-produced motorcycles, as an example.

Tariff rate quotas allow a specified quantity of goods into this country at a reduced rate of customs duty during a specified period of time. There is no limit on the amount of product under this policy, but product in excess of the quota being allowed a special rate would have to pay the normal, generally higher rate.

## EXAMPLES OF COMMODITIES CURRENTLY SUBJECT TO ABSOLUTE QUOTAS*

- Animal feeds containing milk or milk derivatives.
- Butter substitutes containing over 45 percent butterfat.
- Buttermix, over 5.5 percent, but not over 45 percent by weight of butterfat.
- Natural cheddar cheese made from unpasteurized milk and aged not less than nine months.
- Chocolate crumb and other similar products containing in excess of 5.5 percent by weight butterfat.

---

*Source: U.S. Department of the Treasury, U.S. Customs Service Publication 519, revised July 1988.

- Ice cream, condensed or evaporated milk and cream.
- Peanuts, milk, cream (fluid or frozen, fresh or sour).
- Certain sugars, asyrups, and molasses.
- Stainless steel bar, rod, and alloy tool steel, tungsten.

Further, absolute quotas are in place applicable only to European Economic Community countries, as follow:

- Sweetened chocolate in 10 lb. or more bars.
- Candy and other confectionary.
- Apple or pear juice, white still wines, ale, porter, stout, and beer.

## EXAMPLES OF COMMODITIES SUBJECT TO TARIFF RATE QUOTAS

- Tuna fish.
- Whiskbrooms and other brooms, wholly or partially made of broom corn.

# CHAPTER 2

# YOU ONLY TALK DOWN TO CHILDREN

## or "IF IT'S NOT KINDERGARTEN, WHY ACT THAT WAY?"

No matter where you travel on business, chances are quite good that you will come across a fellow American with a camera around his neck, a baseball or club team hat on his head, and perhaps even a wife with a beehive hairdo created only the day before in Paris when she should have been touring the Louvre. The only words not in English that these souls will know may be *matinee* or *pasta* or *Gezundheit*, and your existence will never be the same should you find yourself in any way with them in your travels.

### OUR ANCESTORS WERE BILINGUAL?

For some perverse reason, within this polyglot melting-pot country of ours, it seems that very few people can speak another language outside our borders; they tend to think "American English" and all of its idioms are some sort of universal language to be understood by anyone if they are spoken slowly and simply enough. Further, it seems that very few people take the time or the discipline to understand the subtleties of their language relative to what other people overseas might have learned under the impression that it was the same language. Put very simply, most non-English speaking people abroad learn what can best be referred to as the "Queen's English" not American English.

Imagine, if you can, what it must be like to think you know English as a second language when an American you meet talks as fast as most of us do, uses as much slang as most of us do, and often interrupts before anyone else can fully answer.

Given this backdrop, how then can you be assured that the language you speak will allow you to communicate overseas to a point where things will get done well and where you might even make a few lasting friendships?

Perhaps some stories will help reinforce the necessity of adequate preparation and comprehension of the issues on both sides, theirs and ours.

### Finnish versus English

One time, on a bus ride from Helsinki to Turko, Finland, to catch a ship for Stockholm, I urgently wished I could crawl under my seat and hide while two other Americans (tourists, I guess) spoke baby talk slowly and loudly to the Finnish driver in the hope he would understand they wanted to stop at a toilet facility enroute!

As the trip developed, you could feel the frustration of the Americans and the gentleness of the Finn driving the bus as they continued in their constant babble and he kept smiling, being polite, and frantically trying to understand what they wanted. A simple phrase book always helps!

### Dutch versus English versus Bad Manners

In Rotterdam in a restaurant at lunchtime, an American businessman at a nearby table insisted to the waitress that "a burger with cheese, fries, and slaw" deserved to be on her restaurant menu in Holland because that sort of food "was necessary to Americans, and was, therefore, *the* best." After a long dissertation on the part of the American with great philosphical rationales to the waitress, she told him in flawless English that she understood every word he had uttered, but that his manners left a great deal to be desired.

## What Happens When You Leave Home for a While?

Too often, Americans travel abroad with expectations that are totally unrealistic; traveling from our culture to another requires a transition in thinking, attitude, and behavior.

Remember that a great many people learn English from people educated in Great Britain; hearing someone speak to you in a language that is not your native tongue is hard enough, but when the person speaks quickly or in silly little expressions, it is even worse.

Stop for a moment and think of the everyday expressions we use. Do we possibly have to be so smug as to think the rest of the world can understand this silliness, or don't we really care? How about telling a Japanese distributor about a customer who *blew you off* over a silly billing error?

How could he possibly interpret in his mind what *blew me off* meant? We do such things all the time without thinking, and our overseas contacts and customers will generally sit and smile at us, not understanding what the point of the conversation is.

Compound this even further by adding regional inflections and accents for Americans in any region of the country, and you will wonder how anything gets communicated.

## "I Cannot Understand the American, but the Japanese Guy is OK!"

I had a problem once in Germany with shipments coming from a Tennessee factory. Contacting our shipping coordinator in Chicago, I asked him to set up a conference call with the warehouse man in Tennessee and to call me back in Wiesbaden.

In Germany a lot of office telephones have a little attachment that allows someone else to listen in next to you while you talk, and our German distributor's warehouse man was eager to hear for himself how the problem would be solved. As we waited for the call, I casually mentioned to him that the shipping coordinator in Chicago was a Japanese-American, and that the warehouse man who would join us in the call was from the southern United States.

The phone rang, and the crystal-clear English of the shipping coordinator came across the line announcing that all parties were waiting to talk. With that, the Tennessee warehouse man chimed in with a classic Tennessee greeting, and I watched the German listening in as he grimaced in confusion trying to understand what he had just heard in "English" from an American!

We discussed our problem, I acted as a go-between for the distributor and the warehouse, and we hung up. My German distributor gave me a pained expression and announced, "I don't believe it. I understood the Japanese man, but not the American man!" The poor guy in Tennessee probably went home and told everyone about his fascinating phone call with Germany, never realizing that he was misunderstood with virtually everything he said: I had acted as his "interpreter."

## CLICHÉS TO AVOID

Pages could be written about what *not* to say. Here are just a few:

- "What falls to the bottom line?" (or any variation thereof).
- "It's just a hop, skip, and a jump from here!"
- "Easy as falling off a log."
- "If I eat anymore, I'll burst" (or "blow up" or whatever).
- "Let's grab a bite."
- "How formal is it?" (Think about the word *formal.*)
- "Where do you want my John Hancock?"

and these aren't the only ones!

## IF IT'S YOUR FIRST TRIP ABROAD ON BUSINESS

My first business trip "overseas" was to Puerto Rico, and while that may sound a bit simplistic, it was a good initiation for all the worldwide travels that were to come. Puerto Rico, a commonwealth that is part of the United States, has its own version of Spanish (laced with English words) and the local currency is the same as in the United States. As a result, issues of exchange and lack of comprehension are vastly reduced. Be assured, people do speak English in this Latin island culture, and you won't go too far astray in your endeavors.

Quite naturally, you can do all of the things in Puerto Rico you do at home: you can easily drink the water; the cars are the same; the laws are quite similar; and your initiation, if you need one, is well placed here or in many other Caribbean countries familiar with Americans, e.g., Jamaica, Barbados, and Curacao. Once you learn the ropes, however, you will find yourself eager to try new places, new ideas, and new adventures in business building.

A word of caution in Puerto Rico: do not discuss independence or statehood with Puerto Ricans; you may never know on which side of the issue your audience stands, and you can find yourself suddenly placed in the role of a tourist rather than a business executive looking for sales if you tread onto this delicate issue.

Further, Puerto Rico has a very weak economy. It has been said it would be the poorest state in the Union if it ever did receive or accept statehood. Yet there are pockets of great wealth and business can be generated. Our annual orders generally exceeded close to $1 million for products with a distributor cost averaging anywhere from $5 to $35 each.

## Other Places Where You Will Feel Immediately Comfortable

Later chapters will talk about Australia, New Zealand, and Great Britain. Unlike your first possible venture, Puerto Rico, the food in those English-speaking countries will be familiar, in general, and the cameraderie will be uniquely appropriate to the way you expect it. Unlike Puerto Rico, however, it will obviously take you a longer time to fly to those countries, and you truly ought to "get your feet wet" before trying the big guys!

In Holland virtually everyone speaks very good English.

While the culture will not always be familar to you, this country too is a good starting point.

### So Far, You're Safe

Puerto Rico, Great Britain, Australia, New Zealand, and Holland will give you an opportunity to test your business acumen without straying too far in uncharted waters, but as we discussed earlier, you will still have to be sure you are communicating clearly, without slang and without buzzwords. You'll even be able to read the signs at the airports!

Then one day you will realize that real business development lies in still other areas of the world where the challenges are greater, but these markets can become your test areas to try different promotional and advertising ideas. (See Chapter 11 for serious advertising and promotion planning on a broader basis.)

## IF YOU ARE REALLY GOOD, YOU'LL KNOW WHEN TO TRAVEL

Making the transition from tourist to business executive requires some degree of skill in determining when it is appropriate to board a plane, briefcase (not camera) in hand, to conduct business in these "starter countries."

First, avoid the Caribbean in August, September, and October unless you want to experience tropical storms and hurricanes. Further, try to avoid the Caribbean during holiday tourist seasons like Christmas and spring break from college. While summer may seem like a ridiculous time to fly south, remember you are seeking business; hotels may be easier to book into; rates will be lower; and you will, in general, be less hassled.

If you live in the Northern Hemisphere, travel to Australia or New Zealand in our winter means you will be there during their summer. A great many people in these countries holiday (vacation) at that time, and prior planning will be critical. Obviously, a trip to Britain would follow the same considerations of watching to avoid high tourist seasons, local vacations, and the like.

## NOW YOU CAN BEGIN TO ACT LIKE A WORLD TRAVELER

Okay, you've accomplished these first steps. Your passport has a visa in it from Australia, the immigration and customs people at Heathrow in London have stamped your passport, you've gone through customs here and have been welcomed home by the local airport agent, and you have not had an opportunity to act like the tourists in Finland described earlier or the businessman in Rotterdam who demanded his burger and fries.

If you are ready to expand into the world in a professional way now, let's begin to look at the balance of this book and the various tables and charts designed to be helpful for planning purposes. Remember, you are going to communicate clearly and with great skill to people who either don't fully understand you or who have learned English in a manner to be described elsewhere in this book.

# APPENDIX

## EXPRESSIONS TO USE WITH CARE WHEN YOU ARE ABROAD SPEAKING TO SOMEONE WHOSE ENGLISH IS NOT THEIR NATIVE TONGUE MUCH LESS "AMERICAN ENGLISH!"

We all tend to pick up slang in our everyday language, and just as the German expression *Er hat keine Tasse in seinem Schrank* would sound crazy translated to us ("He has no cup in his cabinet"), so too must we be careful in terms of what we say to others. The German expression by the way means "He is crazy!"

Think carefully before you burst forth with anything like these:

"I have to *catch* a plane."

"You've put me *in the hot seat.*"

"*Cool it,* I'll be ready soon!"

"That's as *easy as pie.*"

"*Watch* your language with the ladies."
"Don't be a *wiseacre*."
"Let me ask you *point-blank*."
"This will sell *like hot cakes*."
"Does he *know the score*?"
"Let's *shoot the works*!"
"Can you *drop a hint*."
"No reason to *fly off the handle*!"
"You really *hit home* with that one."
"Stop *beating about the bush*."
"That's a *load* off my mind!"
"Be careful, he might *take a powder*!"
"*Net, net*, that's it."
"He'll work his *fanny* off!" (NEVER say this in an English-speaking country like Australia!)

The same thing, by the way, can be said if you learn another language and people do the above to you in their language, the one you think you have learned!

# CHAPTER 3

# TRADEMARKS ARE HOLY

## or "IF YOU DON'T PROTECT IT, YOU LOSE IT"

If there is one thing in any product which we tend to take for granted, it is generally the product name, its trademark. Curiously, that name was probably in place before any of us became involved with the company or product. Someone somewhere conjured up the name, and most of us are simply corporate heirs destined to help perpetuate the success and the franchise surrounding the name, the trademark. Once in a great while, we have an opportunity to participate in the creation of a new trademark, but in any event, there are rules of the game, here and abroad, in terms of how to protect that name.

When I began my business career as a very young man at Procter & Gamble, we were told early in our jobs that the brand name we worked with was sacred. We were told never to use the product's name in any advertising play on words or pun, never to incorporate the name in any way in any effort which would tend to diminish the importance of the trademark. All of the money invested over the years on behalf of each brand's franchise was at stake, and we were to protect the brand at all costs.

You can imagine what a rude awakening I had years later when I was sent sample tennis racquets made in Taiwan and marketed in various markets trademarked with the name *Head* when that name belonged exclusively to my employer at the time, AMF. We had no manufacturing arrangements in Taiwan at that time; in fact, one selling point for the product then was its exclusive U.S. manufacture. Trying to deal with that apparent infringement on the trademark was to be a story with virtually no ending, but it was not unique.

On my first business trip to Australia, I discovered that a Sydney merchant had registered a trade name for a product which was identical to one I was about to sell in that market. Our "friend" had registered the name in anticipation of my arrival, and he planned to ransom the name back to our company for a handsome figure. He wanted $10,000 to resell our own name to us.

Sadly, in the overall scheme of things, the man in Sydney had no product with our name, just a fraudulent hold on our trademark and an interesting scheme to make a quick killing on an American company eager to establish itself in his country. Further, the Taiwanese product was a clear-cut counterfeit of a product Head had discontinued a few years earlier; the product had limited sales appeal because the counterfeiter was not current in terms of product availability, but the issue of trademark infringement still existed.

## HOW DO YOU ESTABLISH AND PROTECT A NAME?

The proper establishment and protection of a trademark, here or overseas, must be preeminent in your thinking, and there are steps to protect your product names and the investment you have in them.

First, be sure to retain the services of a reputable international law firm. Never rely simply on someone with legal training; a background of significant experience is of prime importance, and it will be well worth your while to investigate various firms before you begin to establish a significant, broad-based overseas selling plan.

Additionally, you will be required to show proof that products with appropriate names have indeed been shipped, sold, and promoted in various markets. You should retain overseas advertising on your products that will detail the timing of product introduction, sale, and market exposure.

Doing this will require you and your international law firm

to review registered names before you go into a truly major effort in a major market. Just as someone might step on your toes, you too can find yourself infringing on someone else's name in a market where you have less than a great deal of familiarity.

## DO YOU WANT TO TRANSLATE YOUR PRODUCT NAME?

Wherever it is possible, use the American name of your product unless it literally translates into something unacceptable abroad.

The story everyone has heard involves GM and its Chevrolet Nova in Latin America. Whether it is true or not, Nova can be interpreted as *no va* or "no travel" in Spanish. No one wants to admit this story is true, but it does point out the type of problems potentially facing anyone going overseas with a trademark.

When you use the U.S. identity of your product overseas, you assure the buyer that this product is the same as the one available in America. There are always importers and buyers who will remain convinced that U.S. companies use export to reduce inventories of unwanted products or to clear warehouses of obsolete goods. As preposterous as this may sound to an honest and sincere business executive, this practice was not uncommon several years ago.

## WHY BE AMERICAN OVERSEAS?

Overseas buyers want to feel they are participating in some American experience by virtue of buying U.S. products. If McDonald's had changed its name abroad, do you honestly believe the Taipei, Taiwan, store would have set a world record for first-week sales with McDonald's?

There is really little question but that people abroad wish to identify with all that they perceive to be great or part of the culture of America. Often, the glamour and allure we tend to take for granted in selling products here can cause an amazingly powerful buyer response overseas. If you disagree with this, reflect a bit on Marlboro cigarettes, their western theme, and the broad acceptance of that cigarette brand literally everywhere.

One of the more mundane products we ever marketed overseas had to be a heavy-duty automobile replacement shock absorber called "Red Ryder." In some places buyers could hardly pronounce the product name, but pictures of the product in a saddle rifle bag with a sheriff's star and other old western adornments made Red Ryder a best-seller everywhere. (In fact, some Japanese competitors wanted the product banned in Japan, claiming the red color distracted drivers behind cars equipped with Red Ryders!)

## PIRATING INTELLECTUAL PROPERTIES

It's generally easy to understand someone copying a product like a tennis racquet. Anyone who has traveled to Taiwan and has been in Snake Alley in Taipei knows about all of the counterfeit watches available with Seiko (and other) movements for $25, and while some of those travelers might have also purchased inexpensive versions of popular U.S. books, I wonder if they ever knew they were buying pirated intellectual property when they did so.

The issue is even more complex: look at Encyclopaedia Brittanica, as an example. The Tan Ching Book Company in Taiwan (Republic of China) is producing and selling a Chinese-language encyclopedia, *Concise Encyclopaedia Brittanica.* They are, in fact, copying a version of the encyclopedia which Brittanica finished for the People's Republic of China in 1986, part of a joint effort with a publishing firm in Beijing.

Apparently, in Taiwan they translated simplified Chinese characters into characters more appropriate for their audience in Taiwan. Further, and as you would expect, they also rewrote the information in the encyclopedia on Chinese history to reflect their own point of view rather than that of the Communists.

An additional wrinkle to all this is that Encyclopaedia Brittanica is working with another Taiwanese publisher on a version of the encyclopedia for that market. The pirate firm has usurped that opportunity for the other Taiwan publisher and for Brittanica with its copy.

In May 1989 a Taipei court ruled that Encyclopaedia Brittanica did not possess a Taiwan copyright because Taiwan and the U.S. trade agreements were broken in 1978 along with diplomatic relations.

## Some Final Rules to Follow

You must register your trademarks if you feel they warrant protection from predators, counterfeiters, and some people looking for a quick profit.

Maintain near-perfect files and records of the sale of your branded products by market, with dates and clear notations of the names used in advertising, the advertising vehicles, sales promotion efforts, an any other situation of market exposure. Reinforce this policy with overseas sales agents and distributors.

Do not allow overseas distributors, sales agents, etc. to create advertising or promotional efforts on behalf of your brands unless you can give final approval and your legal people pass on the effort as well. One way to handle this without creating an aura of distrust with your overseas people is to create booklets or sheets of approved advertising and promotional formats for all overseas use.

Remember that various languages will require different amounts of space within your advertising and promotional materials. While you can provide sample ads in English with great ease, consider the addition of sample ads in other languages common to markets where you expend reasonable marketing efforts. This also gives you a chance to guarantee what your message ought to be before someone tries to rewrite it! Anytime someone decides he or she has "a better idea" for your advertising or promotional effort, you run the risk of trademark problems or liability claims. You should always assume final responsibility for what is said, and you should be sure legal counsel has approved the claims and the use of your trademark.

## Laws Governing Trademark Infringement

Laws governing trademark infringement have truly evolved and been refined over the past century. The Paris Convention of 1883 may well be looked at as a starting point in deciding that unlawful trademark use and/or unlawful indication of country of origin are the burden of the contracting country, the buyer, to insure prohibition of entry. In fact, the importing country has the right to confiscate these illegal goods. While there have been conservative reactions to this ruling in ensuing years, the United States at a Madrid conference in 1890 asked that the law be loosely redone to assert only that the importing country should simply prohibit importation of goods in this category.

Instead of trying to be a backwoods lawyer, you need to keep in mind the following regulations:

- All goods illegally bearing a trademark or trade name shall be seized on importation into those countries who are signatory to this agreement and where such mark or name has a right to legal protection. Most industrialized and developing countries of the world are in this category that calls for seizure, but if you have a problem such as one that might occur with Taiwan, you need to be aware of it.
- Seizure shall likewise be effected in the country where the mark or name was illegally applied or in the country into which the goods bearing it have been imported.
- Seizure shall take place at the request either of the public prosecutor or of any other competent authority or of any interested party, whether a natural or a juridical person, in conformity with the domestic law of each country. When illegal Head tennis racquets appeared at the docks on the West Coast, or when counterfeit Rolex watches were blatantly advertised in newspapers in 1984–1985, someone should have acted!
- The authorities shall not be bound to effect seizure in transit.
- If the law of a country does not permit seizure on importa-

tion, such seizure shall be replaced by prohibition of importation or by seizure within such country.

- If the law of a country permits neither seizure on importation nor prohibition of importation nor seizure within the country, then, until such time as the law is modified accordingly, these measures shall be replaced by the actions and remedies available in such cases to nationals under the law of such country.

### Clearing Your Mark

Most countries have very specific laws that protect existing brand names and marks of products manufactured within their countries. An international law firm should work with your lawyers to insure you are not inadvertently violating someone else's laws in the same way you would want to be protected if a product appeared on our shores with your name or a very close variation!

# APPENDIX

## TRADEMARKS/COPYRIGHTS AREN'T ALL— A CHECKLIST OF ILLEGAL ACTIVITIES YOU SHOULD BE AWARE OF

Too many times, an export opportunity has been lost because a new exporter became frightened by the competition's price practices or marketing thrust or any number of other things, some of which are illegal and should be brought to the attention of the U.S. Department of Commerce and even of your Congressional representative. Following is a short list of things you can and should know about in doing business abroad:

1. *Dumping is unfair.* Dumping means less than fair value and/or cost of production in pricing when a product is sold for export outside its home or producing market.

2. *Deceptive pricing is illegal.* Advertising or otherwise promoting a fictitious price to eliminate or diminish buying interest in other like products is clearly illegal.
3. *False labeling or mislabeling is unfair and illegal.* Mislabeling any low-quality product in a manner which suggests a higher or improved quality is simply illegal in international trade.
4. *False advertising.* In addition to the unfair use of advertising claims which are false, the use of "patent applied for" and "patent pending" when the user doesn't even have a patent application filed, is against the law.
5. *Product copying or simulation.* International law has decreed that any manufacturer who knowingly copies a product so as to mislead the buying public into believing it is identical and/or is produced by the same company, is violating the law.
6. *False designation of origin.* Put very simply, you must tell where a product was produced, and you clearly cannot contrive to establish another location of origin.
7. *Articles produced by foreign monopolies, nonmarket economy countries, or prison labor.* Such articles may not be unfair and illegal in export. While it is generally agreed that any or all of the above may make the existence of an unfair trade practice more likely, these do not if they stand alone.
8. *Exclusive sales contracts are not unfair practices.* At this time exclusivity in and unto itself is not unfair or illegal.

# CHAPTER 4

# CONTRACTS CAN BE FOREVER

## or "HOW DO YOU FIND A GOOD PARTNER WITHOUT GIVING AWAY THE STORE?"

We have all been taught to rely on our laws and to believe that a contract is a contract. The only problem is that *our* laws may not always be *their* laws.

This chapter is not intended to replace the substantive advice of good legal counsel; you will always run the risk of being trapped in a very bad situation at one time or another, if you don't have a good lawyer helping you to understand why our laws may differ from Spanish-based laws and even from French, Napoleonic Code laws, i.e., common law here versus civil law elsewhere, precedential proof versus codes and established rules.

### PITFALLS, PRATFALLS, AND OVERALL EMBARRASSMENT

First, consider the good news: in almost every country where English is the spoken language, the legal system bears a great similarity to the one with which we are accustomed. This is only appropriate since each country in this category evolved its systems from Britain and British common law.

The bad news is "the other guys." Spanish-speaking countries, for example, have a legal system based on a series of codes or civil procedures, and so too have France, Germany, and many other European countries. (It will be fascinating to watch the

European Economic Community (EEC) deal with these traditional differences after 1992.) Asian countries, Japan for one, the People's Republic of China for another, differ in still another manner. Their contractual documents, while probably very straightforward in content, quite often begin like some sort of old-time love letter. Proclamations of mutual good faith, admiration, and concerted joint efforts are seemingly always the preamble in a contract generated in Japan or China.

Do not, however, find yourself lulled into any degree of complacency by the rhetoric of friendship, mutuality of interest, common bonds of success, and spirit of comradeship in these contracts from Japan and/or China. Your wording of "best efforts" will gain you nothing in return.

## Major World Legal Systems

Most of the countries of the world can be categorized into one or another legal system: common law or civil law. Civil law forms the basis for the legal systems of western Europe, most of Latin America, parts of Asia, and Africa. Common law, as mentioned earlier, is British-based, and is the legal system under which we and all English-speaking countries operate. The socialist countries of the world, generally civil law countries, have been evolving to what will assuredly one day be a distinctively different system from the two we will discuss. Finally, there are countries you will want to deal with where the legal system is based, in whole or in part, on something which probably can be called customary or religious law. These countries are the fundamentalist Moslem countries plus Israel and India.

Now that I have given you cause to fear the worst, let me advise you that over the decades, the differences among these systems seem to have become less significant; each system has taken from the other, and has become somewhat of a blend, reflecting the changing needs of populations and the world as a whole. To oversimplify the difference between common law and civil law countries, civil law countries deemphasize cases as a solution, relying more on statutes, decrees, and existing legislation. Judicial decision making, therefore, becomes less important than in common law countries where we hope to plead a case based on the experiences and results of others with some perspective on past decisions and their relationship to our problems at hand.

## Saying That Should Be Enough

You are probably right, but for every generalization there are major exceptions: In France high court decisions are very important, yet France is a civil law (Napoleonic Code) country. The state of California, we are told, has more codes than some civil law, code countries!

If this subject intrigues you enough to pursue it further, the book *How to Find the Law* by Morris L. Cohen and Robert C. Berring should be on your reading list.

## European Labor Laws

U.S. business executives can be confronted with concepts and practices well beyond their knowledge when they become involved on the continent with laws totally unknown in this country. Even maintaining a basic knowledge of the labor laws in some continental European countries will not provide the necessary understanding of the dynamics of labor relations, for example, in Holland or Belgium or Germany.

Over the years various collective bargaining processes have altered and modified the laws in many of these countries; the process in some cases seemed oblivious to the actual laws on the books at the time.

Each country has its own system of labor relations practices, and broad-based policies on your part might have devastating results for you and your company if you are not careful!

## Employee Termination as an Example

I'm not a lawyer, and this book is not a legal document, so the issues of human resource problems, in total, can best be served by legal counsel. Termination of an employee is worth discussing, however, since the concept of job security, per se, has become classic European policy.

European laws to guarantee job security are deep in the entire social system of the continent; they are founded in politics, industrial relations, and economics going as far back as World War II. While there may not always be uniformity among countries, many cross-cultural influences exist. With the EEC, this will be reinforced even further.

In addition to severance payments, concepts of security for employees may also include priority in rehiring and even the possibility of government takeover of a business, temporarily or permanently, plus plant management by the workers themselves.

## What's the Basis for This?

A contract exists between worker and management in which the worker is willing to subordinate his or her role to the command of the employer, and this does not require a written document; it can be implied. European labor laws recognize this "subordination of roles" and protect the employee against abuses.

## What Does It Mean if You Want to Hire a Work Force?

Basically, it means there are strict regulations governing termination and people's rights to work. You can expect intervention from local or national government bodies if you take action which oversteps the status quo between worker and management—and tips the balance of power, if you will.

## And Unions?

Unionization does not appear to be on the wane in Europe as it is in some areas of this country. Unions are generally pressured by factions from two different sides in Europe, the left and the right. The left will demand stronger control over private business, and a higher degree of intervention and regulation from both the union and the government.

## What's a Quid pro Quo?

The most rational way to negotiate through a contract where both sides (if they are rational) will be satisfied, is to offer what is generally referred to as a "quid pro quo" or "something for something." Thought of in another way, there should be some thing or things in contracts which give both sides the opportunity to feel they have obtained what they wanted.

Examples:

- With the People's Republic of China, we had a venture where our equipment and their labor manufactured inflatable sports balls, e.g., soccer balls, basketballs, footballs, etc. We reserved the rights to all export sales and purchased production from the factory. They, in turn, had the right to sell output exclusively within their own country.
- With an Australian distributor, the contract term was three years, but the renewal was to be negotiated at the end of the second year, allowing the distributor the third year to sell down his inventories of our products if we wanted to terminate that distributor. If we opted to renew the contract, we would add on years starting after year two.

## A Contract Is the Company, Not You!

A good contract between good partners should last well beyond your tenure in office or even that of your overseas partner. There should be something there to protect future participants to continue or amend (or even cancel) without recrimination on either side, and both sides should always feel they are being dealt with fairly.

That's the last "philosophy" you'll get in this chapter.

## Want to Deal in a Spanish-Speaking Area?

Be careful when you arrange an agreement with a sales representative or distributor unless you can prove substantive wrongdoing or fraud or inadequate performance in the courts of your agent's or distributor's country, you will surely have great difficulty in getting out of a contract.

You can assign an independent sales representative to a sales responsibility in the country where he or she resides, but in the courts of that country even a simple letter of understanding or agreement may be interpreted as a binding contract. Although you may want to replace the representative, he or she may decide your grounds are not sufficient.

As simple as that sounds, while you and the representative argue the validity of any arrangement and whether or not he or she is owed any commission, the lawyers of the representative can arrange with the port authorities (legally) for any and all goods you ship in—even if sold by someone else or destined for someone else—to be impounded at the port of entry and/or the commissions to accrue to the "former" sales representative. All this can take place unless you have followed the letter of the law in that country prior to establishing the relationship. Local law firms in each place, or branches, are a great help in such cases.

## How a Contract Might Protect You

Once we had a distributor in Japan. It was our first, somewhat naive, experience in Japan, and this distributor was not exactly first-rate. Our distribution contract with him, however, was quite clear, and one condition forbade his selling our product anywhere outside of the territory we had agreed upon, i.e., Japan.

He purchased product from us at a very good price, but was not totally able to succeed in business with us. One day we received a message from our distributor in Finland, telling us that our product was becoming available in Finland through some external source, and that the prices were very, very low. That external source was the Japanese distributor who had shipped the product across the Soviet Union into Finland in an effort to clear his warehouse and his books. On the surface the situation would seem quite clear: contract violation. It was, but read on.

We had refused a provision in the contract of this Japanese distributor that would have given him an opportunity for inventory adjustments with us in the event the business got sour or changed somewhat in terms of what could be sold. Lacking any such provision, was he not in some way justified, at a later date, in telling us and our new replacement distributor that he might simply dump the merchandise on the local Japanese market if we didn't try to work with him in disposing of it in an orderly fashion?

What sort of quid pro quo exists where one partner in a contract has his back to the wall, and is forced to take steps that cause undue problems in order to protect his business?

## What about "Best Efforts" in a Contract?

We worked through a British intermediary once to sell the Soviet Union some very specialized equipment the Russians wanted to check welds in the natural gas pipeline they were constructing to Western Europe. The Soviet Union seems always hard-pressed for Western currency, and the deal was made with the Russians asking if we would take heavy machinery in trade. The compromise was that we would exert our "best efforts" at accommodating them with the heavy machinery, provided one of our subsidiary companies wanted those goods; otherwise, the Russians would be required to pay in dollars.

We did indeed try to settle the account with machinery, but Russian technology is a bit behind that of other countries in the design and operation of some machinery. Simply put, no one wanted their lathes and grinders, and my mission was to go to the Soviet trading company in New York to tell them we had expended our best efforts, but that we now needed dollars. This sort of dealing puts both sides in adversarial positions where neither believes the other, and where future deals are often colored by the suspicions of previous misunderstandings.

## One Way to Find a Distributor and Worry Less

The U.S. Department of Commerce operates something called the Matchmaker Program. The focus, of course, is to help U.S. companies in the development of overseas business through overseas Commercial Officers who work to identify the best match between interested parties in this country and abroad.

According to the Department of Commerce, a limited number of potential countries are selected each year based, in part, on the results of various global surveys and the recommendations of overseas U.S. personnel. From these evaluations a theme is developed that uses end-user sectors in the markets to help provide introductions to U.S. companies. Participation is limited only to those executives empowered to sign agency or distribution agreements.

U.S. Foreign Commercial Service Officers located overseas in the appropriate markets evaluate each company's marketing prospects and then work to develop private individual appointments for each firm. This is a dating service that is very serious and important! Matches are also developed where joint ventures or licensing agreements can best serve our interests.

The Matchmaker event takes place in an appropriate business facility, and a portion of each Matchmaker event is left open to walk-in trade to insure for every possible contact. Commerce does this so well they can even help you with hotel suggestions for your visit as well as reasonable air fares!

## What Matchmaker Provides

The following points are detailed in the Department of Commerce publication on Matchmaker services:

- Detailed briefings by industry experts and our Commercial Service Officers.
- Arrangements for individual appointments.
- Promotion of participant products and services to potential distributors and sales representatives.
- Open meetings with selected and matched key distributors and sales agents as well as other commercial contacts, all tailored to meet the specific objectives of you, the participant.
- Publication of an official catalog for use by the overseas industry before, during, and after your visit.

- Arrangement of an official reception where participants can meet socially with local business and government leaders.
- Arrangements for adequate support staff to help each participant.
- Assistance in evaluating a representative or joint venture or licensing arrangement to help you avoid some of the pitfalls existing in some overseas countries.

## How Do You Become Involved?

The Department of Commerce, (202) 377–3181, can send you a packet that will ask you to sign a participation agreement, pay a very reasonable fee, describe what your product(s) and goals are, include a 250-word statement about your company and its product for an official brochure, and send 25 sets of your company's sales literature for pre-show promotion and as an aid to the matchmaking process. Some of my earlier export experiences used this system with good success in Japan and various parts of Latin America.

## OK, Now How Do I Qualify a Customer?

Obviously, there are several ways you can verify the legitimacy of those who represent themselves as what you need to succeed abroad.

First, you should always feel free to contact the foreign embassy or consulate of the country in which you are interested. The commercial attaché should be willing to assist you in any way possible. You should also ask a potential distributor or partner for his banking connection, and then ask the U.S. office of that bank to assist you.

A reasonably good business library, with reference books and directories, might be able to provide you with insights into a company if it is large enough. The U.S. Department of Commerce and the World Trade Centers Association both have resources to assist you in evaluating the worthiness of a new partner.

## SUMMARY

There are a great many rather subtle issues involved in working with people overseas, but there are also a great many resources available to you to insure that you don't give away the business with the wrong contract or by having your goods impounded in some port until an issue is settled.

Most of the time, you will be dealing with conscientious, hard-working people who will share some part of your dreams and goals. Use our government resources whenever you feel an issue is in question, and be sure you have capable legal advice to handle matters that involve different cultures and economic positions.

# APPENDIX

### AGENCIES WHERE YOU CAN FIND HELP FOR A VARIETY OF NEEDS

The following partial list of government agencies is provided to deal with the general issues we all face as exporters who might encounter business competitors and situations that are illegal, unethical, or simply not fair. Don't hesitate to contact these agencies:

1. International Trade Administration, (202) 377–1780. These people enforce antidumping statutes, subsidized goods, and goods allegedly sold at less than fair market value.
2. U.S. International Trade Commission, (202) 252–1003. An agency to advise Congress and the president on tariff policy and foreign trade; works to assure fair tariffs on imported goods.
3. U.S. Trade Representative, (202) 395–3204. Primary trade negotiator overseeing the application of remedies to unfair trade practices.
4. U.S. Court of Appeals for the Federal Circuit, (202) 633–6550. Reviews decisions of U.S. Court of International Trade on classifications and duties on imported goods.

5. International Trade Administration, (202) 377–2456. Monitors and analyzes foreign investment in this country.
6. Overseas Private Investment Corporation, (202) 457–7000. Provides political risk insurance, direct loans, and loan guarantees to U.S. private investors qualified to support their corporate investments abroad. We used them with AMF when we put our inflatable ball manufacturing equipment into China in a venture to produce balls, by using our machines and Chinese labor.
7. Treasury Department, (202) 376–0395. Has authority under Trading with the Enemy Act and the International Emergency Economic Powers Act to control financial and commercial dealings in times of war or emergency.
8. Inter-American Development Bank, (202) 623–1000. Through loans and technical assistance, this agency promotes the investment of public and private capital in member nations (Latin America, Yugoslavia, some western European countries, Japan, Canada, and Israel) for economic and social development.
9. International Bank for Reconstruction and Development (World Bank), (202) 477–5606. Funded by loans from private capital markets, it encourages investment in underdeveloped and developing countries.
10. International Finance Corporation, (202) 477–5606. Promotes private enterprise in developing countries with investments in projects that establish or expand businesses.
11. Caribbean/Central American Action, (202) 466–7464. Promotes trade and investment in Caribbean Basin countries.
12. National Association of Manufacturers, (202) 637–3146. Represents the manufacturing sector of the U.S. economy in international economic issues.
13. Export/Import Bank of the U.S., (202) 566–8990. Aids in financing exports of U.S. goods and services.
14. International Trade Administration, (202) 377–3181. Counsels U.S. firms on programs of U.S. Department of Commerce to improve export.
15. Pan American Development Foundation, (202) 458–3969. Provides developing countries in Latin America and the Caribbean with financial and technical assistance for economic and social development.

# CHAPTER 5

# WHAT GOE$ UP OFTEN COMES DOWN

## or "THERE'S MORE TO WINNING THAN TODAY'S EXCHANGE RATE"

Other chapters of this book have stressed product quality, differentiation with competition here and abroad, your endeavors to communicate with overseas associates, ways and means of selling, advertising, and promoting, and the development of good manners with a sensitivity to another culture and language.

While these can be major criteria for long-term success, the price levels at which you and your overseas partners decide to establish a business will often be the adhesive to hold the relationship together during the vagaries of exchange that will surely occur over the years.

### EXCHANGE RATES AND THE DOLLAR

In 1973 it took 12.5 Mexican pesos to equal a dollar; each peso was worth 8 cents, and that exchange rate was solid into 1974 and 1975. By 1986, however, the exchange rate had risen dramatically requiring 923.5 pesos to equal a dollar; each peso was worth one-tenth of a cent. While the Mexican saga may be a bit extreme, think about starting a business in Japan in the mid-70's or Japan building one in the United States.

In 1974 the average exchange rate with the Japanese yen was about 300 yen to 1 dollar. Anytime a Japanese wanted to buy an American product, consider the transaction to be one where he (women aren't as yet too popular in Japanese business transactions) would have to "give over" 300 of his yen for each U.S. dollar charged. If an American product was being sold for $5, the seller would receive the equivalent of Y1500. In 1975 the exchange rate averaged 305. While a rate like this might make it less favorable for American products in Japan, it is interesting to note that this was a wonderful opportunity for Japanese automakers to sell their cars in this country. It coincides with the time when Nissan and Toyota were expanding their presence here.

With a 300:1 exchange rate, a vehicle that might have cost Y550,000 in Japan would have had an equivalent value in this country of about $1,850! If the exchange rate was 130:1, as it has been recently, Y550,000 would have been over $4,200! Any wonder that the success of a product can often be tied in some measure to a favorable exchange rate? When you add in a product that was over-engineered because the Japanese automobile manufacturers and their culture were totally adverse to failure, you have the start of a winning market! While markets have been built under less favorable circumstances, if you are edgy over entry into a market, a rate that favors you is an extra advantage not to be overlooked.

## Other Markets, Other Values

To convince you that rate alone is not a sole determinant for success, however, we began a very profitable business in Australia when the exchange rate meant every U.S. dollar in product sold there cost Australian buyers only 79 percent of their Australian dollars; last year, those same buyers, because the rate had changed, needed to spend 121 percent of their dollar to buy $1 U.S. in product made here. Along the way, the business in Australia exceeded $2 million in sales on products with an average unit value of about $5 U.S. and an exchange rate that seemingly always favored the buyer rather than the seller until relatively recently.

While consideration of exchange rates is an item requiring a great deal of negotiation early in the development of an overseas business relationship, there are further items necessitating somewhat of a change in the way you think when you operate solely in this country and everyone is operating with the same currency and laws.

Conducting business in this country, in terms of pricing policy, is reasonably uncomplicated compared to exporting, thanks, in part, to the Robinson-Patman Act, which precludes unfair competitive practices dealing with price and price-related matters. Overseas each market can be its own universe where you can price on a market-by-market basis, but there are local laws on import prices in some places. While there may be a temptation to run rampant, and to want to unload excess inventories at low prices, there are local laws to discourage you and to protect local businesses.

## Pricing on a Market-by-Market Basis

Market-by-market pricing allows you the opportunity to recognize economic differences among countries. It lets you realize solid profit levels in industrialized countries, and it allows you the opportunity to develop a franchise for the long run if you wish to do so in emerging and undeveloped areas where future considerations may be important for competitive or other reasons, and price can be a constraint if it's too high. Of significance in all of this, however, is the fact that there is no "blanket policy." The laws in some countries are very specific about protecting local manufacturing from dumping, whether you consider what you are doing dumping or not.

## Local Laws

One such law of fair pricing in New Zealand, for example, covers comparable domestic value or CDV. You cannot price some products going into a CDV market at a price below that charged to similar customers in the country of manufacturing and exporting origin. If you are challenged, you had better be prepared to explain and justify your pricing.

While CDV is quite clear in its definitions, your pricing policies, even though apparently fair, can cause a furor in other markets if and when domestic manufacturers feel you may be dumping in their market because your prices appear to be "too good." The line you have to walk is a very fine one, and being too aggressive with pricing practices can often be dangerous, while being aggressive in marketing and promotional activities can surely be better in building a franchise.

With all of these considerations, how then can anyone establish prices that do not violate any laws and protect both buyer and seller from the apparent vagaries of exchange rate fluctuations? How can you establish pricing policies in Australia, New Zealand, Hong Kong, Mexico, Germany, Switzerland, Great Britian, Malaysia, or anywhere else? What needs to be done for near- and long-term protection of both parties and to establish growth conditions so that a product line can flourish?

## Hedging on a Contract

In the short run one method may well be to stipulate, in an initial agreement or contract, and/or in subsequent pricing discussions, that the selling price you establish will remain in force unless the rate of exchange, as noted on a specific contract date, varies plus or minus by an agreed upon percent. This then tells both parties to the agreement that there is a range in which both of you agree to operate, but that if that range becomes stretched too far in either party's favor, you both will renegotiate to bring things back together. You must remember that selling and distribution arrangements with overseas companies are partnerships. When both sides respect each other, and when no one realizes a distinct advantage over the other, both sides benefit.

What can you do, however, when exchange rates begin to spiral in an uncontrolled fashion? Let's take as an example Mexico or Argentina, where rates of exchange from one year to the next are extremely volatile; such countries will offer a different set of situations.

## Using Alternatives to the Dollar

One possible action might be to source products to be sold in a market area from a third country where exchange rate gyrations are not quite as volatile with the customer country. Further, you may wish to consider taking payment in the local currency or in local market goods as barter or countertrade.

Local currency will require that you seek a place to ultimately put the funds or convert those funds for your use. Buying local advertising or having a sales meeting in the market may be ways to use the proceeds of a sale when you cannot convert the currency into dollars. Barter adds a dimension to the extent that you will then have to find a buyer in order to recoup your cash. These are the risks of dealing with less stable markets, and you will ultimately have to decide if the risk is worth the reward.

Further, if you again consider the value of product quality, and if you have done your work well in establishing a product franchise based on sound product values, the importance of prices may not vanish. But it will surely be less significant when rates fluctuate than otherwise would be the case. Proof can be found in the things we often take for granted.

## Quality versus Price

McDonald's has thrived in Japan through exchange fluctuations where the yen is three times stronger than it once was versus the dollar. Conversely, Toyota and Nissan have spread their risk only slightly by building cars outside Japan as well as in that country. But in these cases buyer perceptions of quality, value, and consistent performance prevail to sustain these companies and their products. Exchange rates will vary, potato prices may fluctuate, and menu prices may reflect some of this, but McDonald's continues to hold a solid franchise in the fast food business worldwide.

## Legal and Cultural Issues

As a separate issue, your prices abroad may often be construed as special discounts, special commissions, or bonus plans. Therefore, you may be careful. A thorough understanding of contractual arrangements and promotional deals can protect you from misunderstanding, product seizure, fines, and even permanent boycott in a market.

Cultures of customers are a consideration not to be ignored in your dealings. Several years ago, we arranged with a German company to have a very thorough product line distributed on a private label basis. We listened at meetings as our new distributor talked about the "family relationship" we both now had, and we shared his comments about long-term sales success, even though he was buying at a disadvantageous German market exchange rate versus the dollar.

We had long serious discussions concerning his initial prices, which were gradually increased over time. One year we felt he was due for a major increase. We asked our European manager to communicate a specified increase to this customer, who became enraged at what he perceived to be our rather cavalier attitude toward "his" prices. We had offered a flat percentage increase to cover every item in the line, regardless of its importance in the market or its sales vitality.

I flew to Europe in an attempt to mend fences. In recognition of this customer's precise attitude about business, I listed every item in his line on a piece of paper along with its individual price history, including the one being proposed. Since each item had its own price based on popularity and sales, it was clear we would have to review every item, one by one.

The market dictated individual-item pricing; every competitor priced that way through the distribution system all the way to the ultimate consumer. Certain variations could possibly change the competitive nature of the entire line in that market. After three months of nearly continuous discussion and negotiation, we finally achieved a compromise. Had our manager taken the time to understand the German market, the customer, and the history of the exchange rate between the German marks and the U.S. dollar, our lives would have been much easier.

Every market and every customer might well have its own agenda in terms of pricing. Continued examination and concern about local laws, rates of exchange, and methods of payment will ease your relationship and ensure the success you want to share with your overseas customers.

In the Middle and Far East, price obviously is essential to a selling relationship, but negotiating has become an art form for the buyer, and it must be done as a rite of passage to prove business acumen to Western sellers. Do not walk away from a good price discussion because you think you are being stalled; it is all part of "the game." Your customers will tell you price understanding is a necessary ingredient to mutual trust. For people in that part of the world, it is just as important as accepting hospitality is. A word of caution, however: don't worry about the buyers' profit level in the Middle and Far East. They will take care of that aspect of the business, and you would be better served to make sure that you can make a profit after you have negotiated with those buyers!

Finally, in any part of the world, watch out for a buyer who never gives you an argument on price. Whenever that happens, you have been too generous with what you have given away rather than earned for yourself and your company.

## The Exchange Rate and Personal Expenses

Never exchange your dollars for the currency of a foreign country, and then take whatever you have left of that currency to a second country and exchange it for the second country's currency. If you continue to do this as you go from one country to another and then perhaps to a third country, you will find that the service charges you have to pay for each currency exchange will slowly erode the value of the dollars you began with. You will be astounded to see how much you have lost when you finally reconvert what is left into dollars at the end of your trip!

The solution is to change some of your dollars in country A, while saving other dollars to change them in countries B and C.

## When the Dollar Is Rising versus Other Currencies

Never change dollars into the currency of the land you plan to visit ahead of time, and don't buy traveler's checks in the currency of the country you plan to visit. For example, if you check the exchange rate for the dollar versus the Japanese yen shown in the table on page 52, you will see that one U.S. dollar in June 1989 bought 140.8 Japanese yen. (By way of contrast, if you had exchanged one dollar in June 1988, you would have received only 132.4 yen!)

Additionally, use your credit cards if you think the dollar

will continue to rise since the exchange rate charged is posted at the time the sale is recorded by the card company. On the table, imagine the 1983 Mexican peso rate as month one of a trip, and the 1984 rate as the month the bill incurred was posted by the card company—a nice discount for you! In fact, charge as much as you can on a trip to a country where the currency is dropping steadily in value versus the dollar.

Banks usually have a better exchange rate than a hotel, so look around before you panic and convert dollars anywhere. Further, you will usually get a better rate in the country you are in rather than the United States, so don't fill your money belt before you leave.

### When the Dollar Is Falling versus Other Currencies

This is a tough situation because things seem to become more and more expensive as you go.

First, if the situation appears to be a steadily declining one for the dollar, convert your dollars to local currency as soon as you can. The longer you wait, the less you will get.

Second, charge as little as possible because the rate you pay later may be worse than what it is now.

## SUMMARY

Currency issues, in general, are complex and worthy of a great deal of study well in advance of a planned trip, for personal and business financial reasons.

In preparing to negotiate prices abroad, try to be as knowledgeable as possible about the relatively long-term performance of the currency you will be dealing with; you should try to develop some sensitivity to how the exchange rates have fluctuated over time and what that impact can mean to you and your customers.

Be understanding not only to your financial needs as they relate to the exchange, but also to the needs of your customers wherever they may be. I think we all tend to look at ourselves as the center of our own universe, and the dollar as the only negotiable currency. Escudos, lire, pesetas, guilders, sucres, francs, and marks are all equally important to the people earning and spending those currencies, so be fair.

# APPENDIX

## EXCHANGE RATES
## A HISTORIC PERSPECTIVE
## (and Why Quality and Service Should Mean More than Price)

If you think entering an export market is an occasional thing, don't try it. Every intelligent overseas buyer on this earth has already met the American manufacturer who tried to sell when the dollar was cheap by overseas standards or who tried to sell simply to reduce inventories. You must look at selling overseas as a long-term commitment to building your sales base, learning how to improve your technology, and to building a real defense against "those guys" coming into your market when you can't counterattack by going into theirs. You can sell against low-cost markets by building extras into your competing product: extra service, extra warranty, extra distribution benefits, extra quality, extra features, and so forth.

The table on page 52 shows exchange rate histories for 22 selected countries over the period 1974–89. If anyone in those countries bought or sold solely on price over that time period, here are some of the scenarios which would have been in plan.

1. If you were a New Zealand importer of American men's underwear in 1974, you were, in effect, buying at a 24 percent discount. Every $100 U.S. in purchases actually only cost you NZ$76.02. In 1975 your discount would have changed dramatically, to only 5 percent, and the $100 U.S. you purchased would have cost you NZ$95.81. By 1989 you would be paying a premium: every $100 U.S. would now cost you NZ$170.94.

**Mr. Kiwi:** Let's hope you were able to convince your customers that our U.S. made underwear lasted significantly longer than the silly things available from Thailand at lower prices, and let's hope your supplier reinforced that point, was very prompt and thorough in his deliveries, and that he even gave you some extra discounts for volume to offset the inflation in your country, which sure cut your overseas buying power.

2. In Japan in 1975, any distributor of U.S. high-performance motor oils for cars was paying Y305 for every dollar of a U.S. product he brought into the country. Today he can double his purchases (if prices have remained constant) because every U.S. dollar now costs him only Y140.

**Mr. Yankee Supplier:** I hope you were supportive and helpful of this customer in 1975 when American prices seemed quite high to Japanese buyers. Good relationships and good friends work with each other in harmony in Japan, and if you played that game, your sales should be extraordinary today!

3. In Singapore, 1975 marked the beginning of the high-tech industrialization of that small country. If you acted as an importer to the United States of microswitches from Singapore when its dollar was 2.3 times ours, and if you were happy with that price, you must be in ecstasy today if you're buying at 1.953 Singapore dollars to ours—that's 16 percent less!

$$$$$$

Look at the trends in the table, conjure up some scenarious like those shown above, then seriously look at your products for export, and determine what non-price features you have versus anyone else that will allow you to succeed regardless of price!

## EXCHANGE RATES 1974–89 (mid-points)

| COUNTRY/CURRENCY per U.S. Dollar | 1974 | 1975 | 1976 | 1977 | 1978 | 1979 |
|---|---|---|---|---|---|---|
| Australia/Dollar | 0.7536 | 0.7955 | 0.9205 | 0.8761 | 0.8692 | 0.9046 |
| Austria/Schilling | 17.13 | 18.51 | 16.77 | 15.13 | 13.37 | 12.43 |
| Belgium/Franc | 36.12 | 39.53 | 35.98 | 32.94 | 28.8 | 28.05 |
| Canada/Dollar | 0.991 | 1.016 | 1.009 | 1.094 | 1.186 | 1.168 |
| Chile/Peso | 1.87 | 8.5 | 17.42 | 27.96 | 33.95 | 39 |
| Peoples Republic of China/Yuan | 1.84 | 1.97 | 1.88 | 1.73 | 1.52 | 1.5 |
| France/Franc | 4.4445 | 4.4855 | 4.9697 | 4.705 | 4.18 | 4.02 |
| West Germany/Mark | 2.409 | 2.622 | 2.362 | 2.105 | 1.828 | 1.731 |
| India/Rupee | 8.15 | 8.9365 | 8.881 | 8.2085 | 8.1883 | 7.9067 |
| Italy/Lira | 649.4 | 683.5 | 875 | 871.5 | 829.7 | 804 |
| Japan/Yen | 300.95 | 305.15 | 292.8 | 240 | 194.6 | 239.7 |
| Korea/Won | 484 | 484 | 484 | 484 | 484 | 484 |
| Mexico/Peso | 12.5 | 12.5 | 19.95 | 22.736 | 22.724 | 22.802 |
| Netherlands/Guilder | 2.506 | 2.688 | 2.457 | 2.28 | 1.969 | 1.905 |
| New Zealand/Dollar | 0.7602 | 0.9581 | 1.0526 | 0.9807 | 0.9376 | 1.014 |
| Pakistan/Rupee | 9.9 | 9.9 | 9.9 | 9.9 | 9.9 | 9.9 |
| Singapore/Dollar | 2.312 | 2.4895 | 2.4555 | 2.3385 | 2.1635 | 2.159 |
| South Africa/Rand | 0.67116 | 0.68963 | 0.86956 | 0.86956 | 0.86956 | 0.86956 |
| Spain/Peseta | 56.112 | 59.774 | 68.288 | 80.912 | 70.11 | 66.149 |
| Sweden/Krone | 4.08 | 4.385 | 4.126 | 4.669 | 4.295 | 4.146 |
| United Kingdom/Pound | 0.4258 | 0.49419 | 0.58741 | 0.52466 | 0.49152 | 0.44964 |
| Venezuela/Bolivar | 4.285 | 4.285 | 4.292 | 4.292 | 4.292 | 4.292 |

| *1980* | *1981* | *1982* | *1983* | *1984* | *1985* | *1986* | *1987* | *1988* | *1989* |
|---|---|---|---|---|---|---|---|---|---|
| | | | | | | | | June | June |
| 0.847 | 0.887 | 1.02 | 1.109 | 1.208 | 1.469 | 1.504 | 1.384 | 1.259 | 1.2987 |
| 13.81 | 15.86 | 16.69 | 19.34 | 22.05 | 17.28 | 13.71 | 11.25 | 12.82 | 13.76 |
| 31.52 | 38.46 | 46.92 | 55.64 | 63.08 | 50.36 | 40.41 | 33.15 | 38.16 | 40.91 |
| 1.195 | 1.186 | 1.229 | 1.244 | 1.321 | 1.397 | 1.38 | 1.3 | 1.213 | 1.1936 |
| 39 | 39 | 73.43 | 87.53 | 128.24 | 183.86 | 204.73 | 238.14 | 249.24 | 256.42 |
| 1.53 | 1.75 | 1.92 | 1.98 | 2.8 | 3.2 | 3.72 | 3.72 | 3.72 | 3.72 |
| 4.516 | 5.748 | 6.725 | 8.347 | 9.592 | 7.561 | 6.455 | 5.34 | 6.142 | 6.6405 |
| 1.959 | 2.255 | 2.376 | 2.724 | 3.148 | 2.461 | 1.941 | 1.581 | 1.821 | 1.956 |
| 7.9302 | 9.099 | 9.634 | 10.493 | 12.451 | 12.165 | 13.122 | 12.877 | 14.11 | 16.42 |
| 930.5 | 1200 | 1370 | 1659.5 | 1935.9 | 1678.5 | 1358.1 | 1169.2 | 1351.8 | 1415.75 |
| 203 | 219.9 | 235 | 232.2 | 251.1 | 200.5 | 159.1 | 123.5 | 132.4 | 140.8 |
| 656.9 | 700.5 | 748.8 | 795.5 | 827.4 | 890.2 | 861.4 | 792.3 | 728.3 | 658.72 |
| 23.376 | 26.23 | 96.48 | 143.93 | 192.56 | 371.7 | 923.5 | 2209.7 | ... | 2491 |
| 2.192 | 2.468 | 2.624 | 3.064 | 3.549 | 2.772 | 2.192 | 1.777 | 2.055 | 2.201 |
| 1.0392 | 1.213 | 1.365 | 1.528 | 2.094 | 2.006 | 1.91 | 1.521 | 1.505 | 1.7094 |
| 9.9 | 9.9 | 12.84 | 13.5 | 15.36 | 15.98 | 17.25 | 17.45 | 18 | 20.8 |
| 2.0935 | 2.048 | 2.108 | 2.127 | 2.178 | 2.105 | 2.175 | 1.998 | 2.041 | 1.953 |
| 0.82686 | 0.74616 | 0.957 | 1.076 | 1.222 | 1.985 | 2.558 | 2.183 | 1.93 | 2.772 |
| 79.25 | 97.45 | 125.601 | 156.7 | 173.4 | 154.15 | 132.395 | 109 | 121.513 | 124.8 |
| 4.373 | 5.571 | 7.294 | 8.001 | 8.989 | 7.615 | 6.819 | 5.848 | 6.253 | 6.624 |
| 0.41929 | 0.524 | 0.619 | 0.689 | 0.865 | 0.692 | 0.678 | 0.534 | 0.585 | 0.647 |
| 4.292 | 4.292 | 4.292 | 4.3 | 7.5 | 7.5 | 14.5 | 14.5 | 14.5 | 38.7 |

source: Moody's International and Northern Trust Bank, Chicago, Ill.

# CHAPTER 6

# OVERSEAS MANNERS/ OVERSEAS JAILS

## or "WHY AM I HERE, MY PASSPORT IS IN ORDER!"

By the time you have reached this chapter, it should be somewhat obvious to you that the central theme of this book and the attitude espoused is one that generally says that American companies with American employees can successfully sell American-made goods overseas. The concept of doing this well goes hand-in-glove with the way successful American (and foreign) companies operate in this country, i.e., quality products, service, responsibility to the customer, and fairness. There is one great flag of caution, however.

### BEING NARROW-MINDED CAN MEAN TROUBLE

It is absolutely and totally possible that the best people in any organization, the best marketers, the best accountants, and the best legal minds—anyone who can help you grow to great levels in the United States—can be totally blind when it comes to dealing with people in another culture. That blindness can put them and you in jeopardy.

Learning to be adaptable and flexible overseas may well be an acquired skill for most people, and most people, we hope, in time will react to the situation in a positive manner that benefits the company and its efforts. Do not, however, expect people to be on the lookout for differences in other cultures that may be danger signs early on.

## Mexican Jails—The Stories Are True

One of our best sales representative in Latin America, who was born in Mexico but lived virtually his entire life in the United States, went to Mexico on a very important trip to negotiate a long-term buying arrangement with a significant distributor. His trip was to negotiate prices for the future at a time when the peso was truly faltering, and he was instructed to follow through on past-due invoices.

For the weekend, he thought it would be fun to visit the ancestral town where he was born and where he believed he still had relatives. His sister had moved back to that town as well, and the trip would be a surprise for her. He then committed mistake number one in Mexico: he rented a car on his own and drove several hours from Mexico City for his homecoming.

Upon reaching his destination and being greeted by old friends, he conservatively drank quantities of tequilla, swapped stories with old friends and neighbors, and then decided it was time to drive back to Mexico City. It was Sunday afternoon, and the bullfights were on in town so there was a lot of traffic. As he neared the outskirts of town, another car ran a stop sign and literally tore off one side of his car. The driver of the offending vehicle got out of his car, looked at the damage, muttered something, and ran away, leaving his car and the damaged car of our representative. Forgetting where he was, the representative stood by the rental car even though onlookers urged him to run away. Finally the police arrived.

Clearly, the accident was not his fault, and there were large numbers of witnesses to attest to this fact, but the police, finding him alone at the scene of an accident, "invited" him to the local police station to "report all of the details." Upon his arrival at the police station, he found himself "detained" in a cell which was, in fact, a holding area for a large number of local inhabitants who were there for a wide variety of crimes, primarily excessive drinking.

As one might imagine, his new-found "friends" were totally intrigued with his presence. He spoke Spanish and looked the way they did, but he was dressed like "a gringo." In fact, they kept calling him *gringo*. No matter how loudly he protested to his captors, no one was about to help him until the local magistrate was available after the bullfights or perhaps even the next day. He was gently advised to enjoy the hospitality offered.

At this point, it seems reasonably fair to comment on Mexican jails and Mexican laws. According to this poor hapless sales representative, as well as others who seem to know, Mexican jails are made particularly unsavory to avoid people using them as homes away from home when conditions in their regular homes are generally pretty bad. Most Mexicans consider their jails with great fear and trepidation as places to avoid at all costs. Thus one always runs from an accident, whether innocent or guilty. For the police, an arrest is the only way to understand and learn the causes and consequences of an accident; there is no reading of one's rights, and no one is innocent until proven guilty.

Fortunately for our victim, one of the witnesses at the accident was a neighbor of our man's sister. His sister knew the police chief, and she went to the bullfights in search of her brother's intended liberator. After a few harrowing hours, our salesman was free and surely wiser. The message was quite clear: do not drive yourself around Mexico, and even if you are only a passenger when there might be an accident, U.S. passport or not, innocent or guilty, leave the scene!

## Things You Never Discuss in Public

We are told repeatedly never to discuss religion or politics with people—especially overseas when the issue may involve their lives—unless you want to end a friendship at one extreme or go away to jail at another.

Kuwait is a melting pot for people from every part of the Arab world. Egyptians, Syrians, Palestinians, and Arabs from all over the Middle East work in Kuwait. Some hotel rooms there supply a Koran as easily as the Gideons provide a Bible here. When things move slowly, as they often do in this part of the world, there might often be a temptation to begin reading the Koran in your hotel room. Moving another step forward from reading this holy book, you might then find yourself tempted to discuss Islam with your hosts. While I take a certain delight in knowing about the five pillars of Islam—the basic tenets of the religion—and while such information is sometimes helpful in a social conversation, the following story, absolutely true, was very dangerous for anyone to pursue, much less an American.

A colleague pored over the Koran one evening; he already knew a little Moslem history, and his curiosity was understandable. Unfortunately, the next day a Palestinian employee of his customer was driving him to the gold bazaar for some last minute gift buying, and the topic of "a return to my homeland" was brought up by the Palestinian. "What homeland?" our American asked with a certain degree of provocation of his voice. The conversation then developed into a broad-scale history lesson concerning Abraham (Ibrahim), the Jews, and the prophet Mohamed's arrival in Jerusalem several centuries after the Jews came there following their journey out of Egypt.

The Palestinian, who had better manners than the American businessman, maintained his composure, finally telling our colleague he would give him some books to read. The message, however, is clear and easy: do not discuss religion and politics anywhere unless you are a carefree, foolish, first-class boor who truly wants to fail.

## Sensitive Issues in Latin America

As we all know, some countries, notably Argentina and Chile, have had rather tumultuous histories involving military rule and large numbers of people who have "vanished." This is something one never talks about in those two countries.

Similarly, opportunities for freedom of expression and open discussion in public places do not always exist in some Latin American countries. People will not be comfortable with you if you try to discuss politics and political issues on a street corner or in a restaurant when their country is run with very strict rules governing behavior.

## They Listen in Too

The year President Reagan was shot, I was in South America and felt I simply had to call home to hear what had happened. It was more than a bit disconcerting, however, when I asked a question and the operator interrupted to ask that the answer be repeated!

During the British/Argentine conflict over the Falkland/Malvinas Islands, a phone conversation with our factory outside Buenos Aires was cut off after our Argentinian contact mentioned that the Argentinians had destroyed the British Navy and I commented that the British had destroyed the Argentinian Air Force.

## SUMMARY

There are myriad situations overseas that enable us to see and learn things of both a business and cultural nature. The temptation to ask provocative questions exists in many of us because Americans, in general, are very much up front and open. We live in a free society where there is no penalty for asking questions. But not all other countries are equally blessed.

Further, the chance exists that you may violate a local law or social rule if you decide to become involved in a different culture without taking the time to learn something of that culture.

Japan, for example, is a country where you may never have a problem provided you exercise restraint in your actions and show patience in your reactions. Latin American countries may give you an opportunity to be a bit flamboyant, but only after you and your overseas associates have gotten to know each other. Yet you will be forced to remain silent on certain political issues.

The Middle East is hospitable, but on its own terms. You must respect the laws of Islam when you are in Moslem countries. Europe can be a great deal like this country, but we need to remember that the Europeans have been buying from us and selling to us longer than probably anyone else.

Finally, don't abuse the situations in which you find yourself. Be aware of subtle differences if you can, country by country, so you don't find yourself trying to remember your Spanish vocabulary in jail or having your camera confiscated for taking pictures of Arab women wearing veils. Don't send sexist calendars to Scandinavia, and don't discuss religion in the Arab Middle East.

Do respect your colleagues who are your hosts for who they are and what they are. If you do so, you will succeed beyond your best dreams. The most enriching part of your business life can be the experiences you gain from meeting people abroad and truly learning about them and their life-style.

*Note:* You will surely meet people overseas who will become great friends of yours. When they visit this country, be sure to invite them to your home for dinner. The opportunity they will have to see how Americans live can only be matched by the opportunity your family will have to meet someone from a different culture with different ideas. Do not, however, let your wife decide to crusade for equal rights for women when a Japanese visitor happens to have his wife with him.

My wife, who had perfectly fine intentions, made a special point one time of serving two Japanese wives before their husbands. In one case the husband took whatever was in front of his wife away from her and served himself. There is a lesson to be learned from this: you can show people how we live, but that does not always mean that you should expect your guests to behave exactly as we behave!

Don't serve Mexican food when Mexicans or other South Americans visit. Do think about serving fish when Asians visit because they often prefer eating lighter meals than we do with our red meat and potatoes. Don't serve ham, pork, or shellfish to Arabs or Israelis since both Islam and Orthodox Judaism prohibit these foods. Do have a good time and don't be overwhelmed—you can always ask people what they'd like!

# APPENDIX

## HERE'S A GOOD STARTING POINT TO LEARN ABOUT FOREIGN MARKETS, LOCAL CUSTOMS, ETC.

## U.S. DEPARTMENT OF COMMERCE DESK OFFICER TELEPHONE NUMBERS

The following telephone numbers, in Washington, D.C., area code 202, represent the desk officers available as country specialists to assist you. This is, in effect, a starting point, and the officer at this number can give you suggestions on catalog shows, ways of matching up with interested parties in the country on which they are specialists, and virtually any other start-up problem you may think of. They are a valuable resource. (Please note that some of the numbers may change over time, but an inquiry to one of them will set you in the right direction.)

| *Country* | *Phone* | *Country* | *Phone* |
|---|---|---|---|
| Afghanistan | 377–2954 | Albania | 377–2645 |
| Algeria | 377–5737 | Angola | 377–0357 |
| Argentina | 377–5427 | ASEAN | 377–3875 |
| Australia | 377–3646 | Austria | 377–2434 |
| Bahamas | 377–2912 | Bahrain | 377–5737 |
| Bangladesh | 377–2954 | Barbados | 377–2912 |
| Belgium | 377–2920 | Belize | 377–5563 |
| Benin | 377–4564 | Bermuda | 377–2912 |
| Bhutan | 377–2954 | Bolivia | 377–4302 |
| Botswana | 377–5148 | Brazil | 377–3871 |
| Brunei | 377–3875 | Bulgaria | 377–2645 |
| Burkina Faso | 377–4564 | Burma | 377–5334 |
| Burundi | 377–0357 | Cambodia | 377–4681 |
| Cameroon | 377–0357 | Canada | 377–3101 |
| Cape Verde | 377–4564 | Cayman Islands | 377–2912 |
| Central African Republic | 377–0357 | Chad | 377–4564 |
| Chile | 377–1495 | Colombia | 377–4302 |
| Comoros | 377–4564 | Congo | 377–0357 |
| Costa Rica | 377–5563 | Cuba | 377–5563 |
| Cyprus | 377–3945 | Czechoslovakia | 377–2645 |
| Denmark | 377–3254 | D'Jibouti | 377–4564 |
| Dominican Republic | 377–2527 | Eastern Caribbean | 377–2527 |
| Ecuador | 377–4302 | Egypt | 377–4652 |
| El Salvador | 377–5563 | Equatorial Guinea | 377–0357 |
| Ethiopia | 377–4564 | European Economic | |
| Finland | 377–3254 | Community (EEC) | 377–5276 |
| France | 377–8008 | EEC Tariff Information | 377–2905 |
| Gabon | 377–0357 | Fench Guyana | 377–2912 |
| Germany (West) | 377–2434 | Gambia | 377–4564 |
| Greece | 377–3945 | Ghana | 377–4564 |
| Guatemala | 377–2527 | Grenada | 377–2912 |
| Guinea | 377–4564 | Guadeloupe | 377–2912 |
| Guyana | 377–5563 | Guinea-Bissau | 377–4564 |
| Honduras | 377–5563 | Haiti | 377–2912 |
| Hungary | 377–2645 | Hong Kong | 377–2462 |
| India | 377–2954 | Iceland | 377–3254 |
| Iran | 377–5767 | Indonesia | 377–3875 |
| Ireland | 377–2920 | Iraq | 377–5767 |
| Italy | 377–3945 | Israel | 377–4652 |
| Jamaica | 377–2527 | Ivory Coast | 377–4388 |
| Jordan | 377–5767 | Japan | 377–4527 |
| Kenya | 377–4564 | Kampuchea | 377–4681 |
| Kuwait | 377–5767 | Korea | 377–4399 |
| Lebanon | 377–5767 | Laos | 377–3583 |
| Liberia | 377–4564 | Lesotho | 377–5148 |
| Luxembourg | 377–2920 | Libya | 377–5737 |
| Madagascar | 377–0357 | Macao | 377–2462 |
| Malawi | 377–5148 | Malaysia | 377–3875 |
| Mali | 377–4564 | Maldives | 377–2954 |
| Martinique | 377–2912 | Malta | 377–5401 |
| Mauritius | 377–0357 | Mauritania | 377–4564 |
| Mongolia | 377–3932 | Mexico | 377–2332 |
| Mozambique | 377–5148 | Morocco | 377–5737 |
| Nepal | 377–2954 | Namibia | 377–5148 |

| *Country* | *Phone* | *Country* | *Phone* |
|---|---|---|---|
| Netherlands Antilles | 377–2912 | Netherlands (Holland) | 377–5401 |
| Nicaragua | 377–5563 | New Zealand | 377–3647 |
| Nigeria | 377–4388 | Niger | 377–4564 |
| Oman | 377–5737 | Norway | 377–4414 |
| Pakistan | 377–2954 | Pacific Islands | 377–3647 |
| Paraguay | 377–5427 | Panama | 377–2912 |
| Peru | 377–4302 | People's Republic of China | 377–3583 |
| Poland | 377–2645 | Philippines | 377–3875 |
| Puerto Rico | 377–2912 | Portugal | 377–8010 |
| Romania | 377–2645 | Qatar | 377–5737 |
| Sao Tome/Principe | 377–0357 | Rwanda | 377–0357 |
| Senegal | 377–4564 | Saudi Arabia | 377–5767 |
| Sierra Leone | 377–4564 | Seychelles | 377–4564 |
| Somalia | 377–4564 | Singapore | 377–3875 |
| Spain | 377–4508 | South Africa | 377–5148 |
| St. Bartholomey | 377–2912 | Sri Lanka | 377–2954 |
| Sudan | 377–4564 | St. Maartin | 377–2912 |
| Swaziland | 377–5148 | Surinam | 377–5563 |
| Switzerland | 377–2897 | Sweden | 377–4414 |
| Taiwan | 377–4957 | Syria | 377–5767 |
| Thailand | 377–3875 | Tanzania | 377–4564 |
| Trinidad/Tobago | 377–2912 | Togo | 377–4564 |
| Turks/Caicos | 377–2912 | Tunisia | 377–5737 |
| Uganda | 377–4564 | Turkey | 377–2434 |
| United Arab Emirates | 377–5737 | USSR | 377–4655 |
| Venezuela | 377–1259 | Uruguay | 377–5427 |
| Virgin Islands (UK) | 377–2912 | Viet Nam | 377–4681 |
| Yemen | 377–5767 | Virgin Islands (US) | 377–2912 |
| Zaire | 377–0357 | Yugoslavia | 377–5373 |
| Zimbabwe | 377–5148 | Zambia | 377–5148 |

# CHAPTER 7

# DO I NEED TO LEARN THE LANGUAGE?

## or "I TOLD YOU I'D DO IT IN FINNISH!"

Americans are always condemned overseas for their inability to speak another language. In a country of 240 million people, all of whom are potential customers for one service or product or another, why is it necessary to speak another tongue?

Chapter 13 will supply some helpful hints and a few choice expressions to insure a bit more rapport and enjoyment on an overseas business trip. But one reason for you to think about serious language involvement is simply that we are now a global economy. Overseas business people come here, and they generally can speak English as their second (or third) language. Furthermore, they are taking away some of our domestic customers, and there has to be a way for us "to bring the battle" back to their market.

### IF YOU CAN'T TELL 'EM, YOU CAN'T SELL 'EM

Chapter 2, in part, discussed language in basic communications and the necessity to speak clearly, without slang, when the listener has a different-than-English native tongue but has the learned ability to communicate with you in English. In every case, conversations must be precise and a bit slower than usual.

Any success in any endeavor relies greatly on communication, yet there are ways we can communicate with others who don't speak our language without always knowing one word of theirs. Each of us communicates with words, but we also convey strong messages by reflecting enthusiasm, interest, patience, sincerity, good manners, sensitivity, and any number of things. Virtually every meeting you attend abroad will include an interpreter on your host's side if he or she feels it is important, and your actions and reactions to what transpires during your meeting will often convey as much as the best language lessons could provide.

## Trying Something Different

Several years ago I was invited to attend a special distributor conference in Finland. Our distributor's customers from all over Finland were going to meet for two days in Helsinki. I was asked if I would be part of the program, and if I would make a few remarks with an interpreter standing by my side.

I eagerly agreed to be there, but when my host asked if I would send my speech in advance of my arrival to enable the interpreter to preview and work with it, I decided I was going to test my own feelings about the distributor, his customers, and the entire country: I advised him I would be giving the entire 15-minute presentation by myself and in Finnish! Interestingly, all I knew how to say in Finnish was "thank you."

The speech was written in English and taken to a local Finnish consular office where I asked if the speech could be interpreted and if the interpreter would then simply but slowly read the speech into a tape recorder left in his office.

The manuscript was beautifully typed in Finnish and the tape was as clear as a bell. I sat on the airplane to Finland, earphone connected to the tape recorder, and listened to the speech as I read it over and over until I could pronounce every word without relying on a phonetic copy. By the time the plane reached Helsinki, our distributor seemed more than slightly dubious that I could deliver as promised. Being playful, I refused to show him the script.

The meetings for the day concluded, and we all reconvened in the private dining room of a supper club. I had spent the entire day hearing speakers in Finnish without knowing one word of what they were saying, and my turn was coming. Dinner ended, the room became quiet, and I approached the lectern to begin with "Dear friends" in flawless and precise Finnish.

The speech covered my own ancestors, who had, in part, come from a Swedish-speaking area of Finland to America. It dealt with the products we were eager to sell to these people. After 15 minutes the stories I told were concluded, and the audience went crazy. My host, enjoying the moment as much as I, decided it was time for one last bit of playfulness. He told me I then had to go through a question-and-answer session with his customers—in Finnish, of course. Thankfully it was a joke, and he made a very special presentation to me, awarding me his version of Finnish citizenship.

## There Are Others Just As Crazy

An old and dear friend recently retired from IBM where he had worked for 31 years—a great many of them in international sales. I once told him my story of Finland; he smiled knowingly because he had done exactly the same thing in Spanish in Mexico! I and others have done this same sort of thing in Sweden, Japan, and Taiwan. As "crazy Americans" we can get away with a great deal!

## There Are Limitations

These techniques of improvising speeches in unknown languages have limitations. Basically they are social techniques, not business techniques, and you really can only use them once in any given location. You can do so to prove your sincerity and to develop friendships, but when business gets to serious dealing, playing games is strictly for amateurs. If you have the time and the skill, learning someone else's language is the substantive way to cement a relationship. A word of caution, however, is in order: learning a language will not automatically give you skills in negotiating business deals in another language. Such skills only come with years of practice.

## Why Bother to Learn a Language Then?

After I had studied Spanish at a local language school, my Argentinian colleagues were delighted that in one year's time I had gone from no ability in Spanish to nonstop chatter about food, the weather, and even bad jokes. People who had felt inhibited around me when they tried to speak English were now relaxed in knowing we could converse in Spanish about a great many topics. When I took a classic American joke one time, translated it into Spanish, and told it to a Venezuelan friend in his car, he almost fell out the door laughing. But neither of us presumed that as a result I was ready to discuss serious business policy.

With enough practice, however, it was possible to learn about our business from local business leaders all over Latin America without the aid of an interpreter, and that knowledge provided insights over the long-run which were invaluable in strategy development back in the United States.

### It Doesn't Always Work Well Though

German is another language I learned—first in high school, then in college, and 20 years later after 142 hours of private lessons. I decided once that my favorite customer in Germany, who was coming to visit, needed a little surprise in the form of a new catalog design in German. Product features of "safety" and "economy" and "comfort" were to be emblazoned in German on the cover. The customer nearly fell off his chair when he saw my efforts—the word *comfort* was the German word for *sexual pleasure*!

### If You Don't Live There

The stories told so far are probably some of the best uses you can make of a foreign language and the ability to learn it unless you live in an overseas location where you hear the language every day.

When you travel abroad, watch the conversation in a customer meeting. Cordiality and friendliness will certainly be expressed in English or interpreted into English for you, but when the discussions become serious, and it is time to be very clear and to the point, watch your customers revert to their native tongue lest there be any misunderstanding on their part between their associates and themselves.

## Summary

No one in international business wants to create a relationship based on any degree of uncertainty; distances are too great, dollar amounts are too large, and time can eliminate an opportunity too quickly.

Don't let a language misunderstanding initiate these problems. Use an interpreter whenever you or your customer feel it is necessary. Write everything down for both sides to review and understand. Be patient and avoid idioms, slang, and regional expressions that may create misunderstanding. Rely on another language only when you feel you have attained a solid foundation of knowledge and understanding as well as a thorough grasp of the subtleties each of us has in our native tongue.

# APPENDIX

## YOU MAY NOT SPEAK THE LANGUAGE BUT AT LEAST YOU CAN MEASURE IN IT!!

**A Quick Way to Convert Weight and Measures**

| *To Convert from* | *Into* | *Multiply by* |
|---|---|---|
| kilograms | pounds | 2.2046 |
| pounds | kilograms | 0.4536 |
| inches | centimeters | 2.54 |
| feet | meters | 0.3048 |
| centimeters | inches | 0.3937 |
| meters | feet | 3.2808 |
| miles | kilometers | 1.6093 |
| pints | liters | 0.4732 |
| liters | pints | 2.1136 |
| quarts | liters | 0.9464 |
| liters | quarts | 1.0567 |
| gallons | liters | 3.7854 |
| liters | gallons | 0.2642 |
| cubic feet | cubic centimeters | 28317.0 |
| cubic feet | cubic meters | 0.0283 |

# CHAPTER 8

# ENGLISH FOR YOU ISN'T ENGLISH FOR THEM, ETC.

## or "WHAT DID I SAY THAT WAS SO FUNNY?"

A great many businesses, in an effort to start their thrust abroad with success and relative ease, tend to focus first on English-speaking countries. After all, we do speak the same language—or do we?

Similarly, Latin American markets are often a favorite target because of proximity and the seeming ability of a great many people in this country to speak some degree of Spanish—or of the Spanish spoken in one or another Spanish-speaking family.

### THIS IS OFTEN A TACTICAL ERROR

Over the years it has become apparent that most non-English speaking people who have learned English, as well as others in lands across the sea where English seems to be the mother tongue, don't necessarily speak the same language we do. The words are the same, but the meanings may not always be the same, and this often leads to both embarrassment and some unusual responses from people.

#### Some Examples Are in Order

Not too many years ago, Chevrolet television advertising emphasized the youthfulness of its owners and the vitality of its cars. One of their lines was that their cars "had a lot of spunk."

We were entertaining a British colleague and his wife in our home for dinner one evening, and after dinner they expressed an interest in watching American television. As fate would have it, one of the Chevrolet commercials appeared. As the line about spunky cars came across the air waves, the British couple looked at each other, his wife blushed a bit, and they began giggling. It seems that in Great Britain *spunk* is a slang word for male ejaculate! Needless to say, this then becomes a word one would never dare use in advertising in the United Kingdom.

## But There's More

In Great Britain, *getting stuffed* is only pleasant when two people of the opposite sex are doing it with each other; hence you must never *feel stuffed* after a good meal in London, Birmingham, or anywhere else in the United Kingdom. Further, to us a *bomb* is a failure; to them, it's a success, and in Britain, Australia, and New Zealand an itinerant is not a *bum* because you sit on your *bum*.

The overwhelming curiosity most people have about Americans obviously includes inquiries about our athletics—baseball, football (which is the word for soccer elsewhere in the world), basketball, and any other organized sport. When some Australian associates one time asked me about American football and my team preference, I boldly announced that I "rooted for the Chicago Bears." They were virtually on the floor laughing—not because of the Bears (there's a team in Sydney called the North Sydney Bears), but because when someone *rooted* for someone in their English, it meant he slept with them!

## The Implications for Non-English-Speaking People

A significant number of overseas people you meet have learned the "Queen's English." British English—the mother tongue if you will—is taught in most overseas schools, and the people you meet and work with who want to speak English with you will have learned it that way. As a result, you need to be aware that English-speaking people in Germany, Scandinavia, Japan, etc.

are not always prepared to fully understand your sense of humor or seeming inability to articulate in what they believe to be English.

If the probability of using the wrong word exists within our own language, add in a wide variety of uniquely American slang, either national or regional, and you will be praying for the best as people either giggle or look peculiarly at you.

## The Wild and Wooly Australians

The closest you may ever come to working overseas with people who seem to share a common desire to move the business ahead without fanfare and formality are probably the Australians. Sadly, with only 20 million of them in a continent almost as large as the continental United States, the potentials may not be as great as you would like them.

Australians speak in as funny a manner as we sound to others, and you may find that great concentration is necessary for a day or so until you fall into their pattern. Thanks to Crocodile Dundee, most of us know that *gooday* is a very common expression in Australia, but in some places Australians have a great ability to take their slang and modify it in a poetic fashion that is colorful to hear, but confusing to understand.

A *poof* or a *poofter* might be someone with homosexual tendencies, but if you don't know that you will never know that a *wooly woofter* is the same thing! *Emma Chissum* is not a woman; it's an Australian asking, "How much are they?" Their *mates* are not their wives or husbands, but their friends, and a *shout* is a round of drinks (one of which you will have to pay for before you leave a pub), not yelling.

*Sheilas* and *birds* are girls, not necessarily women, and a *venue* is a location. Don't ever discuss the origins of the country beyond making a casual remark that the American Revolution caused George III to change his policies from sending convicts to America to sending them to Australia.

## What Happens When They Come Here?

How would you like to come here from Britain or Australia, for example, feeling confident that there would be no language issue of any consequence, only to hear that *pop* in the Midwest is *soda* on the East Coast, or that a *submarine sandwich* in one place may be a *grinder* elsewhere, or that what you thought was a water fountain was, in fact, a *bubbler* in some other part of the country? The classic, of course, would be a *New York cut steak* in Chicago and the same steak in New York called—what else—but a *Chicago cut.*

## Problems with Spanish

You will undoubtedly think that it would be the easiest thing in the world to find someone who speaks Spanish to help you all over Latin America. If English is not English everywhere, be assured that Spanish is not Spanish everywhere either! For example, the Mexican word for a baseball cap is not the same word in Argentina. In fact, the Mexican word is a part of the female anatomy in Buenos Aires, where it is used crudely as slang.

## And in Japanese

You should know that there is both a male *and* a female form of the Japanese language, and that it apparently sounds quite silly when a Japanese male hears another man speaking "female" Japanese. One interesting example of these differences is the male Japanese word for *toilet*; no self-respecting woman would ever utter in public the same word the men use!

## What Can We Learn from This?

The net effect of these subtle and not so subtle differences in what appear to be basic languages is that you must be cautious and highly articulate with people from other countries when and if you deal or even socialize with them in English. The contents of this chapter are not intended to inhibit or frighten anyone from going abroad and trying to communicate. Virtually every instance of supposed miscommunication discussed in this chapter gave me a chance to build upon a growing relationship with someone else because we saw the humor in our differences.

The lesson to be learned, however, is that you must avoid being "lazy" in your own language skills. You should not try to negotiate a business arrangement with someone in an offhand or casual manner, and you should try to remember where you are—among people who want to be your friends, but not in a local restaurant or bar in Chicago, San Francisco, Portland, or Cleveland!

# CHAPTER 9

# WAIT, WAIT, AND WAIT

## or "THEY SURE DO THINGS DIFFERENTLY THERE!"

If you haven't traveled a great deal overseas, you may not be fully aware of how much Americans seem to be in a hurry. This can be an asset or a detriment to your dealings, depending upon each situation and country where you find yourself, and it is important to keep this in mind.

To be a bit facetious, when the speed limit on interstate highways was 55 m.p.h., most of us tried to drive with one eye on our rear view mirror and one straight ahead at 65 m.p.h. When the limit was raised in rural areas to 65 m.p.h., we all picked up to 70 to 75!

Henry Ford realized that the best way to produce cars for a mass market was to develop an assembly line, and he and his engineers were constantly reviewing the process to speed things up. The concept of *fast food* was born, nurtured, and matured in this country with McDonald's, Burger King, and every other firm seeking to produce a quick and, we hope, an inexpensive meal for breakfast, lunch, and even dinner. Domino pizza promises delivery within 30 minutes of the time an order is placed.

At airports Americans hurry from their planes only to wait for their luggage. Once they obtain their bags, they hurry to get a cab. Overseas, Americans are always first in the cab lines and last in the airport bus lines. Everywhere American businessmen and businesswomen travel, they create the impression that all they want to do is get to their hotel quickly, unpack, and get to work with their customers and clients. There is an obsession about "the deal" even after normal business hours when (believe it or not) some people relax and get to know each other.

It seems that there is no other country in the world where people want to act as quickly as we do. In some places our apparent desire for speed and efficiency is quite often seen as impatience or as crude, unmannered, and even a bit barbaric behavior, yet it does rub off on some others once in a while.

## A "Corrupted" Japanese

A former Japanese business associate of mine was transferred to the United States for two and a half years, and a year or so after his return to Japan we had a reunion in Tokyo. I was surprised to hear that he was not terribly pleased to be back in Japan, and I was quite curious to hear what it was that he missed in the United States.

"If I go to Narita Airport," he commented, "and there is a long line of people waiting patiently in line at a counter, the last thing that enters my mind as a Japanese is that I should run to the front of the line, pleading that I will miss my plane if I wait. In the United States, an action taking a passenger to the front of a line for any reason causes a loud, vociferous reaction from everyone else. In Japan the people in line may well think terrible things about my behavior if I move to the front, but they will never say anything. I can no longer deal with this politeness after two and a half years in America!"

## First Lesson in Politeness and Patience

Politeness and patience, in spite of all that seemingly surrounds you, are the focus in Japan, in particular, and in a great many other countries, in general. In spite of what you may be conditioned to think, you will not be considered "laid back" or disinterested, if you behave in a fashion proper to the country where you are operating. In the Orient and especially in Japan, business has to "unfold" while a relationship is developed.

The first encounter I had with this attitude was during pricing and distribution negotiations I had in Osaka with a new Japanese distributor. Our customer had teams of people we had to meet during the day and early evening. A member of the first group would pick us up early at our hotel. About midday he and his colleagues would leave the conference room, to be replaced by a second group. Toward dinner time a third group would emerge.

Each negotiating group had a specialized role in the meeting. One was concerned with finance, another with distribution, still another with sales. They realized that our schedule was very limited, and they opted to overlook their normal custom of developing a relationship slowly in favor of trying to accommodate us Americans by squeezing every agenda item into one day. Unfortunately, they never explained their reasoning because they simply thought that they were acting like Americans. We interpreted their actions as highly pressure-laden.

## The Chinese Can Be Flexible If You Ask

In the People's Republic of China, you may well negotiate with the same group or committee, day in and day out, before you come to a resolution. While they may invite you to join them in a dinner banquet, they will retire early, and their interest in early evenings is quite different from the Japanese, who seem to enjoy staying out late.

It is worth noting, however, that if you tell your Chinese hosts that you only have a specified number of days to make an arrangement, they will endeavor to schedule the meetings in accordance with that timetable. One trick I was shown in this regard was to suggest that your plane ticket was for Day X when, in fact, you might have two days more before your ticket was actually booked. This gave you an opportunity to control somewhat the flow of negotiations, knowing you had an extra two days at the end if you needed them. Further, if things ended on time you could perhaps change your ticket and go home early! (A word of caution: only do this if you are prepared to taxi all over Beijing, Shanghai, or wherever you are to change your ticket yourself.)

## Differences between Chinese and Japanese

Both cultures will present you with an opportunity to learn new ways of negotiating. The Japanese may want to spend many days in discussion. They will start very slowly, and only accelerate when they feel a relationship has been established, and that they know you and have some degree of trust.

The Chinese will spend days to insure that they and you truly understand the implications of everything in each deal. In addition, they will spend some time away from you, reviewing what has been discussed with the bureaucracy of the party and their system.

Other countries in Asia will follow the pattern of the Chinese and Japanese, but to a greater or lesser extent, depending on which country you are in. In any case you should not expect to negotiate anything quickly.

## Be Prepared

When you consider the amount of time you will have to spend in negotiations, you will surely see that you must do a tremendous amount of preparation prior to a visit to Asia. Never believe you can enter into discussions of serious and important nature without arming yourself with files and information concerning every conceivable aspect of cost, competition, strategy, and whatever will be necessary to make both parties happy they have spent the time, energy, and patience on the discussion. If you can arrange to bring an interpreter, you will show the seriousness of your intentions, and may even expedite matters a bit by creating an environment of mutual understanding.

## Things Are Different in the Middle East

Most Arab businessmen consider bargaining to be a way of life. Hospitality will be the keynote of your experience in this part of the world, but behind all the dining and comments concerning good friendship, there will be a cunning individual waiting to bargain with you more sharply than almost anyone you have ever met.

As is true in the Far East, the Middle East will require you to know every possible element of your product before you begin to talk in earnest. Any hesitation or bluffing on your part will not be considered merely as a weakness but also as an act of bad faith.

## But There Are "Blunt" People in the Middle East

The Israelis will not require you to stand on any ceremony. They are truly tough and will try to exact every bit of bargaining strength early in the game. Happily, when the day is done and/or after you have made your arrangements, Israeli hospitality and friendship will be as richly rewarding to you as anyone else's.

## What about Latin America?

Time implies quality and sincerity of interest in virtually every Latin country. If something is done quickly, the implication is that it may not be done well or with sincerity. This even includes meeting people because they may consider promptness as a sign that someone merely wants to get things over and completed. You should be prompt for meetings, but don't become aggravated if your host is late.

For your efforts in Latin America, try to remember that for your host nothing good happens quickly. Be prepared to spend a lot of time at lunch or dinner, and be resolute in your determination to get to know your potential customers in a relaxed manner. Think of it as a cigar where the smoke curls deliciously and slowly upwards while the smoker takes careful and long draws on the cigar while leaning back, relaxing, and acting a bit macho.

## Want to Succeed in Australia/New Zealand?

You may be able to come to a conclusion in your negotiations a bit faster in this part of the world, but then the Australians and New Zealanders will expect to spend some time with you in cementing the relationship through a solid bond of friendship. Don't shake hands and run!

It will be necessary and important for you to sit back with your hosts at their office, club, or a restaurant for an evening of "consolidation," where you have to get to know each other socially even though it might mean whiskey without ice! Business will be over, and friendship will be the order of the moment when stories can be told and shared.

## . . . and in Europe

You should find things very similar to the surroundings of Australia or New Zealand: civilized and in order, with a time and a place for everything, including business and social matters.

As with people in other parts of the world, Europeans will want to get to know you. In a way that will be comfortable and familiar for you, Europeans will expect to conclude dealings for the long run. You should enter into a sales effort in Europe as the threshold of a new business friendship in which your partners will want your confidence and trust as much as you want theirs. While this is equally true in other parts of the world, for most of us the culture of Europeans is one with which we have a great deal more familiarity.

Remember, however, that most Europeans will expect you to respect the fact that their society is older (it is), that it is more dignified (whether that's true or not), and that it is more refined (whether or not you want to believe it).

### European Niches

Germans and Swiss will expect you to know every technical aspect of your product. Further, if you are working with them at a very high level, you had better be in a position to make sure your word is your pledge.

Scandinavians, Finns, Danes, and Swedes, in particular, may seem a bit less motivated than their continental counterparts. This may be the result of their strongly socialistic governments and often a cradle-to-grave attitude about life resulting from their government policies.

The British are as varied as their country, but a British friend will truly be a friend forever, provided you keep your word. Acting refined and "gentlemanly or gentlewomanly" is very important in England—less so in other parts of the United Kingdom.

In Italy, enjoy the food and be patient. If there truly is a Roman temperament, it exists where it should, in Italy. The pace will be cordial, but a bit slow due, in part, to a certain amount of posturing by your hosts to assure you that their hospitality and country are second to none. It's fun.

In France, take time to let your host know you recognize the architectural and artistic beauty of the country. Don't ever expect to be invited home, however!

### What about the Russians?

Working with Russians requires a different sort of patience, one that results from your understanding that they have been operating under a system so different from ours for so long that they may not understand your subtleties and vice versa. Again, patience and reason will ultimately be your best tools for success.

## SUMMARY

"Wait, Wait, and Wait" may be a bit trite, but it is to the point virtually anywhere in the world where you may care to operate. Although our cultural differences with other countries have narrowed dramatically since the end of World War II because of high-speed air travel, television, the broad distribution of motion pictures, and myriad other social and political entities, cultural patterns run deep and must be respected.

You will never be faulted for going too slowly in your dealings anywhere in the world. But haste may indeed cause waste that can never be recaptured so that you can then attain a prosperous business arrangement. Be patient in the belief that whatever you and your overseas hosts establish will be long-lasting and often free of some of the more temporal aspects that seem to affect American dealings today.

Just as customers in foreign lands often seem to show a greater loyalty to their suppliers than some of our customers do here to our suppliers, so too will your overseas associates deal with you, provided you maintain a special quality of service, fairness, and patience with them.

# CHAPTER 10

## PRODUCT INTEGRITY, HERE AND THERE

### or "QUALITY *MEANS* QUALITY AND FAIRNESS"

Once upon a time in a land we all know, a corporation president made the prophetic statement that he wanted to be "the low-cost producer" of his industry. He made several public announcements to keep his stockholders happy, and he and his staff created a special cost-reduction program with the engineering department. "I'll pay a bonus for every suggestion we use to reduce cost," he told his engineers, and they merrily set out to find ways to cut cost.

Curiously, there was a marketing department in the same company (an earlier president had announced once that he wanted a "marketing-driven company"), and they were merrily counting the revenue increases produced every year through the sale of the company's product on a worldwide basis. The marketers had done ample product research to determine exactly what it was that consumers wanted to buy, and the product sold was exploiting every positive benefit it had while the competition was running to catch up.

Sadly, no one had told the marketers what was happening with the engineers until customer complaints began to arrive. By then it was too late, and our little company in a land we all know is no more.

## WHY BE A LOW-COST PRODUCER?

It is probable that the idea of trying to be a low-cost producer in any industry accelerated dramatically with the advent of relatively inexpensive foreign goods to our shores. No one seemed to care that a Japanese factory worker and his family lived on a different standard than his American counterpart, or that the economy of a Third World producer country was totally different from ours. The important point was that the "stuff" coming from "their country" was cheaper and we had to compete by lowering our costs, and, in some cases, our quality. In retrospect, that surely was an oversimplified response to a much more serious problem of productivity and quality, but we'll talk more about that later.

### Why Is Low Cost Secondary?

The midpoint of the Japanese yen/U.S. dollar exchange rate in 1975 was 305 yen per dollar; now it is in the 140 range. Presumably without the effects of inflation everything here from Japan should now cost about twice as much as it did in 1975, all other things being the same.

Looked at differently, if you presume the Japanese car industry gained a foothold in this country because they were the low-cost producer in 1975, what is the explanation today? We are told that Japanese automobile engine and transmission technology now exceeds that of American manufacturers. These, among other things, are seemingly what helps that particular Japanese industry in spite of the fact that most American vehicles, model for model with the Japanese, are probably cheaper.

## QUALITY AND SERVICE WILL WIN EVERY TIME

Think about things in your own life, such as items you buy for yourself and your family. When is price the determining issue in your purchase behavior? It probably comes into play only after you have decided which item is the best and most reliable, and after you have made a judgement concerning quality and service versus price. What are some of the issues that face us in the future if you and I want to compete here and abroad against foreign-made goods?

## Some Examples of Quality and Innovation

Jaguar, the automobile manufacturer, went through a very tough period when buyers perceived the cars as excellent in design but poor in quality. Then the people at Jaguar developed a philosophy called *total quality management.* They realized that quality, as a concept and an operating issue, had to affect the entire organization in its attitude and behavior. Quality inspection, as it had been utilized, was truly a poor substitute for getting things right the first time.

Since the early 1980s Jaguar has made enormous strides to return that corporation's image to one of very high quality and reliability. First, they researched owners of their cars and those of competitive vehicles, and in so doing they found 150 major quality problems that had to be dealt with if the firm expected to survive.

Jaguar then established a cross-section task force of managers in a variety of responsible roles in the company to find solutions of lasting worth. They had to reestablish worker pride in the job at hand, and they had to install tougher standards for both employees and suppliers. Realizing that people in the factory were the ones where responsibility for quality had to truly start, Jaguar introduced quality circles among workers and reduced the number of quality inspectors. Quality was to be the workers' focus! Jaguar believes its quality circles work because its leaders feel technical and production issues are ultimately part of a human equation. Yet other cultures still seem to resist this approach.

The German shop floor is still, in great measure, operated by someone telling people what to do. It is further complicated by immigrant workers in some factories, who are not part of the overall culture of Germany. Their interests lie often solely in earning a living rather than in producing a quality product.

Large numbers of Jaguar buyers are now interviewed every month to ensure that both cars and dealers provide satisfactory performance, but also to see what might still be lacking in the vehicles that are purchased.

While this procedure is innovative for Jaguar, Honda, the Japanese manufacturer, has been practicing it for years. Managers must recognize that in this era of global and niche marketing, where subsets of customers exist on a global basis in large and profitable concentrations, innovation and constant product review for improvement are vital ingredients in both near- and long-term success. Some products, notably high-technology information systems, show us where we can compete effectively against others if we remain aware of how our customers use these products.

Customers in high tech tend to refine and alter what they buy. They even develop other systems which often enhance or bypass the standard package they have purchased. While the Japanese, for example, have superb strength in selling standardized products, companies that recognize the need for customer innovation to supplement standardized items can be innovation leaders who demonstrate recognition of their customer needs.

In effect, managers in both the field and central office have to be flexible and understand the constantly changing needs of their buyer/user base if they want to compete and win.

## THE ISSUE OF SERVICE MANAGEMENT

I am reminded of the amazingly fast turnaround time we had in the automotive replacement shock absorber business when we increased our sales abroad nearly 15 fold in 5 years. Whenever a customer needed a product to fit a vehicle in his market but not the U.S. market, we would obtain a competitive product sample from the customer. Often we designed and built our product within eight weeks. It seems that service, as a key ingredient in the selling equation, will always be present if you expect to succeed.

Service is a competitive edge to such an extent that it no

longer can be considered a policy; it is a product of a thriving organization unto itself. One company with far-flung sales maintains 500 parts and distribution locations throughout the world and guarantees delivery within 48 hours. If the firm fails to deliver in two days, the component ordered is free to the buyer!

### Look at the Implications of Service

If you have a support system to truly satisfy customer needs quickly, and if it is well developed with a good information-reporting system, you then enhance your quality image when you interpret the data received on these shipments and recognize the early stages of a problem.

Being proactive rather than slowly reactive means you care about what you are producing and selling, and it means you can express to your buyers a genuine interest in their welfare (and obviously yours).

## THE PATENT ISSUE

Why do Japan and other Asian countries dominate the production and sale of consumer electronics in this country? Or cameras? Or videocasette recorders? Can we believe that research and development in this country have dropped off in favor of short-term profits by American manufacturers?

If you look at the numbers, the percent of U.S. patents issued to residents of foreign countries has risen dramatically since 1974. In 1974, 25 percent of the U.S. patents issued went to foreigners; in 1988, that number was 48 percent of the U.S. patents. Nearly two and a half times more went to Japanese than to Germans; the Germans were double the British; and the following table reflects the fact that we are relinquishing a great deal of the future:

### Who's Doing What?

According to the U.S. Patents and Trademark Office, while U.S. companies are filing patents for oil wells, fishing, trapping, ver-

**Ten Corporations Receiving the Most U.S. Patents**

| *1978* | | *Number of Patents* | *1988* | | *Number of Patents* |
|---|---|---|---|---|---|
| General Electric | United States | 820 | Hitachi | Japan | 907 |
| Westinghouse | United States | 488 | Toshiba | Japan | 750 |
| IBM | United States | 449 | Canon | Japan | 723 |
| Bayer | West Germany | 434 | General Electric | United States | 690 |
| RCA | United States | 423 | Fuji Film | Japan | 589 |
| Xerox | United States | 418 | Philips | Netherlands | 581 |
| Siemens | West Germany | 412 | Siemens | West Germany | 562 |
| Hitachi | Japan | 387 | IBM | United States | 549 |
| DuPont | United States | 386 | Mitsubishi | Japan | 543 |
| Philips | Netherlands | 364 | Bayer | West Germany | 442 |

source: Intellectual Property Owners Inc.

min destruction, packaging, amusement/exercise devices, and games, the Japanese patents are covering photocopying, optical and phonographic recording, photography, electronic plotters, and magnetic disk and tape recording.

### The American Camera Store

A few years ago we went to buy our youngest daughter a new camera. The new thing in cameras at the time was instant load and automatic focus—the whole thing that made picture taking absolutely foolproof. The cameras we were shown were all Japanese, and when I commented to the proprietor that there ought to be an American camera with all those fancy features, his answer was fascinating.

He claimed that market researchers had been in his store years before to determine what the public wanted; quite naturally, he felt the research had been conducted all over the country. His final remark, however, was devastating, "The research was for Japanese clients; I have never been queried by Kodak on anything my customers might want in a camera."

## RESEARCH AND DEVELOPMENT

While nonmilitary research and development expenditures represent about 1.8 percent of the U.S. gross national product

(GNP), our friends in Japan spend nearly 3 percent of their GNP and West Germany invests about 2.6 percent on research and development. In relative terms it can be argued probably that the absolute dollar levels are different, but if patent issuances are any indication of the focus in research and development, someone's priorities have gone a bit astray.

## What about Standards?

Various countries in the world have "standards" or what might be better explained as specific definitions of how products must be manufactured for sale within a country. For example, there are very specific standards in Germany and Great Britain covering the way various electrical components are designed and built. This is generally true in every European country, and is an issue that should become perfectly uniform after the EEC is truly functioning.

The April 17, 1989 issue of *Forbes* described in alarming terms the extent to which the United States has seemingly abdicated its role with respect to standards in various countries in favor of the standards set by Japan and Germany.

The article discussed Saudi Arabia, a major importer of American goods, and a country with very rigid standards on a wide range of products. According to *Forbes*, the United States has allowed itself to "be outflanked. Japan, the U.K., Germany and France have sent teams of standards professionals to Riyadh to advise the Saudi Arabian Standards Organization (SASO) on its 16-year old project to develop product standards." SASO will ultimately produce 42,000 standards on items as diverse as the shelf life of lamb to the color ground wires will have to be in an air conditioner.

Because other countries assist in the development of these standards, do you believe any of them will favor us for any reason other than pure chance? This is astounding given the fact that this country is clearly a major manufacturer of virtually anything the Saudis buy, yet we may not have any influence on the standards they ultimately develop for products.

## A Different Kind of Integrity

Once, a few years ago, I thought there was a chance to work with a U.S. manufacturer of chemicals for swimming pools who was considering exporting his products to Australia. A third party put us together, and we spoke by conference call.

"Yes," he agreed that there was a great market for pool chemicals in Australia, but he was afraid to try because "the Japanese are already selling there." He then admitted that his potential distributor was afraid they would fail because the Japanese prices were so low they seemed to be below their home market price. If that was indeed the situation, it would be a clear case of unfair trade practices, and either the Australian distributor or the American manufacturers should have contacted the Australian Customs or the U.S. Department of Commerce. According to the manufacturer, neither he nor his distributor "wanted to make waves." Therefore, he concluded that he would give up all thought of exporting to Australia.

## Is Everyone Fair?

Probably not, but what else is new? In the automotive replacement parts business, we began to develop a solid market in a country for a shock absorber line whose product was painted red. Because we had to compete with two or three local manufacturers, our development time was quite long, but we finally established a relatively stable market niche and a good business. Our local competitors then tried to have the law changed, claiming the red painted shock absorbers on the rear of a car were a distraction to the driver behind that vehicle. If we consider that the red product was sold in a significantly large number of other countries, this move was preposterous, and the intent of our competitors was vicious. But their claim, if sustained would have been a truly unfair act in trade.

## What Is Super 301?

Super 301 is a section of the U.S. Omnibus Trade and Competitiveness Act of 1988. Designed to break down barriers to entry or business development for U.S. exports, it has caused a great deal of consternation here and abroad. Of course, there may be trade barriers of significance in Japan precluding a reasonable market development for U.S. exports in a wide range of product areas, for example, cigarettes, leather, pharmaceuticals, telecommunications items, and super computers. Further, some people feel that the Japanese distribution system is designed to establish barriers against outsiders. Other observers feel that Western Europe with its EEC zeal has gone too far with its subsidies on agricultural products.

Super 301, by virtue of its existence, may help open new markets or previously protected markets. But it could also cause reverberations and protectionist reactions that might restrict our exports as well as the imports from other countries that now enter the United States. Super 301 allows unilateral retaliation against any country that restricts imports of any U.S. goods. White House trade representatives are supposed to identify any patterns of unfair trade practices involving specific countries.

A list of these "bad guys"—that is, the offending countries—is then supposed to be sent to Congress. At that point efforts to remedy the situation are supposed to be expended through mutual discussions between the United States and the so-called troublemaker countries. If the other guys don't concede, the law dictates U.S. retaliation, probably in the form of increased tariffs, quotas, or even the negation of trade agreements.

## SUMMARY

Product quality, integrity, and service will clearly separate the survivors from the has-beens in the future, and the way we perceive our corporate cultures will be the key to success. While we all want our corporate entities to be growth-oriented and results-oriented, somehow we have to find a way for work to be fun for the people involved. A corporate sense of mission and vision that considers the employees' needs and dreams will surely go a long way in this regard; each company is its products *and* its employees. If we share a sense of mission and an overall vision, we can establish a sense of confidence that can be pervasive in a corporate culture. This exists at IBM today—a company that recognized that change was necessary to its survival.

American industry has too long maintained an adversarial relationship with its unions. While neither side is pure and sweet, both must work together in offering employees challenges, the opportunity to take initiative, and the chance for a reward commensurate with risk. Additionally, everyone in an organization must be made to understand that growth and security come from maintaining an awareness of the ultimate customer who pays the salaries of the producers with his or her purchases.

You should try hard to emphasize results rather than process. While the United States has pioneered a great many processes, including mass production, the results in terms of quality *and* employee satisfaction seem to have been lost somewhere.

As mentioned earlier, integrity and fair dealing with everyone involved in your business are the only policy that will reward you in the long run. You need employees to produce quality products; you need suppliers to sell you quality components!

Finally, we should all foster greater creativity and innovative behavior in our organizations. As managers, we have to reserve the right to reject an idea for a good reason. But to stifle an idea out of hand makes no sense in a competitive world where all of us should be encouraged to care and comment about the job we are doing.

# CHAPTER 11

# ADVERTISING AND SALES PROMOTION OVERSEAS

## or "WHAT A CRAZY WAY TO BUILD THE BUSINESS!"

Someone once told me that the best way to understand the culture of a country was to watch its television. Advertising, it was explained to me, reflected the heart and soul of a country. Thus, understanding it was the surefire way to learn how to communicate in that market when it was my turn to advertise my products there. Since television was more graphic and alive than other media, we felt we could learn the culture faster by watching it than by trying to read newspapers or magazines.

In establishing criteria for good advertising in various parts of the world, the following simple differences seemed to emerge.

## JAPANESE BUYERS STILL NEED CELEBRITIES AND EMOTION

Since Japan is always on everyone's consciousness, we should probably begin there. Celebrities as authorities seemed to imply that fame and fortune in Japan would be important credentials to insure product success.

Further, Japanese advertising appeared to appeal especially to the senses. It was less overt in extolling product qualities, and it endeavored to create an aura around a product. Being explicit was taboo, and music played a key role. Japanese advertising is more designed to appeal to the poetic nature of its audience—a mattress ad, for example, might show people resting on clouds, but it would never compare its coil spring count with that of a competitor.

That was wonderful, but what did it mean for automotive shock absorbers, tennis racquets, water filters, or microswitches? Read on to find the answer!

## SIMILARITY? THEY'RE ALL DIFFERENT!

In Europe, quality and value for money seemed to be the keynote whenever I could understand an advertisement. But there were great differences among France, Germany, Great Britain, and Scandinavia. France seemed to require more of a flair and a bit of flamboyance compared to Germany. The Germans ran all of their ads together, which made it awfully hard to be competitive. Great Britain was clever in its approaches and, as I remember, the Scandinavians didn't even have any television commercials. (If they did, the commercials sure weren't memorable!)

## FINDING A REAL SOURCE OF HELP

Relying on an advertising agency, especially the overseas branch of a U.S. firm with which I was familiar, seemed the best answer in the long run. We coordinated our efforts through the U.S. office, and my inputs represented the initial thrust toward doing what was appropriate in any market of consequence. The overseas offices of the U.S. agency implemented the strategies and supplied the necessary local feeling. There are very solid foreign advertising agencies as well.

## ADVERTISING AGENCIES WORLDWIDE

Most Americans probably do not realize that the Japanese agency Dentsu has evolved from firms founded as far back as 1901. Among the agency's earliest clients are the Matsuya department store, Shiseido cosmetics, and a Japanese soap company now owned by Procter & Gamble. Dentsu has over 3,000 clients today and a mastery over Japanese media that must be considered whenever a foreign company attempts to place ads through any other agency. No wonder Dentsu bills nearly $7 billion annually!

Another powerhouse in the international agency business is Saatchi and Saatchi, which is headquartered in England but worldwide in scope, including several U.S. offices. Saatchi and Saatchi controls nearly $5 billion in annual billings and is represented in this country by the following formerly independent firms: Backer Spielvogel, Ted Bates, Campbell Mithun Esty, and Rumrill-Hoyt. All of Saatchi's holdings, full and partial, produce an annual billing level of over $11 billion.

## ADVERTISING IN CHINA

Even the People's Republic of China, hardly a free-enterprise society, has discovered not only the value of advertising agencies, but the extra worth of agency representation abroad through its Shanghai Advertising Corporation. What do you think of an agency that can represent a market of over 1 billion people? We are told that most Chinese advertising does not emphasize a brand name or attempt to build an image in the same fashion as Western ads might. Their advertising seems to simply announce a product with a very simple explanation. A look at any of the Chinese trading company catalogs clearly reflects that impression.

While Shanghai Advertising has now opened an office to help develop business in the United States, American firms represented in China include Ogilvy and Mather, Young & Rubicam, and McCann-Erickson.

## GOVERNMENT CONTROL OF ADS

If good agencies exist in most major markets of the world, why shouldn't life be easy in terms of advertising development? Just as there are policing bodies in this country to prevent overt fraud and deception, foreign governments reserve the right to preclear advertisements in a variety of ways.

Prescription and nonprescription medicines require government preclearance in Australia, Austria, Denmark, France, Hong Kong, Italy, Mexico, Norway, Paraguay, Singapore, Spain, Taiwan, the United Kingdom, and Venezuela, but not in the United States. Cosmetics advertising requires preclearance in Canada, Mexico, and Taiwan, but not in the United States. In some markets prescription drugs can be advertised only to professionals and the trade. In Egypt, they may be advertised only in medical journals.

## SALES PROMOTION AS AN ADJUNCT

Simply put, sales promotion allows you an opportunity to get closer to the actual buyer than probably any other means of sales development. In this country sales promotion is represented by contests, drawings, in-store displays, and many concepts and ideas that bring together seller and buyer faster than advertising. If you decide that sales promotion is something you wish to pursue, look at the differences in the following Practices that are legal versus illegal in Europe:

- Mail coupons are acceptable in Belgium, Denmark, France, Holland, Italy, Spain, Sweden, and the United Kingdom; they are not legal in Norway, and may or may not be acceptable in Germany!
- Mail-in sweepstakes cannot be used in Belgium, Denmark, Italy, Norway, or Sweden; France, Germany, and Holland will allow them.
- Using merchandise prizes to dealers is illegal in Germany and Norway, but it's OK in Belgium, France, Holland, Italy, Spain, and the United Kingdom.

Refunds, allowances, special buying terms, sampling to consumers, and special factory packs are all legal or illegal in varying degrees worldwide. While American promotional techniques and styles are appreciated and productive abroad, you must be careful to know what is acceptable before you sacrifice your franchise needlessly.

## HOW DO YOU KNOW WHAT PRICE IS FAIR?

In any advertising or sales promotion, there has to be some way to determine if you are being overcharged or if you are truly getting what you pay for. In general, it is not a problem. European print advertising—both in newspapers and magazines—is highly structured and absolutely legitimate in every respect. Rate cards are genuine, and I've never seen any skullduggery with prices or placement of an ad.

We ran a series of advertisements, however, in several Latin American countries for a few years. In some instances the paper simply didn't make it out to its readers each day. While that situation presented its own set of problems, the publishers generally were quite prompt in telling us and refunding our money. A magazine ad caused us a different problem when someone tipped off our competitor that we were going to run a coupon ad with a very attractive price discount for purchase. We were quite surprised to see our competitor's ad in the same issue since neither of us had ever used the magazine prior to that time!

Southeast Asia and Japan were places where we noticed that things weren't always what we thought they should be. You must be sure to have a way of monitoring your ad efforts in those areas. In some Asian markets, Thailand, for example, our advertising agency was quite concerned about getting involved in any advertising without having a strong local presence. The agency's representatives were told quite bluntly that whatever rate we would be quoted would probably be inappropriate. In fact, we were advised that if we paid the printed rates, we would assuredly be the only advertiser ever to do so.

If this kind of behavior exists, you can believe that its twin, the kickback, is right there as well. In Latin America we began finding our ads in every conceivable publication—dog show programs and cookbooks as well as on billboards in some of the most remote roads I'd ever driven on.

## WHAT'S THE SOLUTION IN A BAD MARKET?

The only surefire method to insure your message is getting across in a place where the business is not totally ethical is to outflank the system and use your own point-of-purchase materials, e.g., counter displays, window posters, and even hand-painted signs on walls! Obviously, you will want to do these in the language of the country.

Further, you have to have a system of policing and reimbursing distributors or other authorized people for the ads they may place on your behalf. But be sure you receive tear sheets and other samples of what they have done before you pay them.

## LANGUAGE ISSUES WHEN YOU DO IT YOURSELF

I remember vividly the time we decided to create our first advertisement for Europe. We had been using a relatively large Chicago-based advertising agency with a national reputation, and it seemed only right and proper that the agency should also do our European ads.

Germany was our first market. We had developed solid distribution with a new product line and wanted the world to know we had "a whole new range of product" in Germany. The translation of the American copy was done by some service bureau, and the ad was inserted into various German magazines. Since we were all very new at this business, we presumed that our agency had screened the ad. We can only wonder if any of the people at the German magazines bothered to look at our great effort. Our German sales manager had not seen the ad prior to insertion, nor had his staff. The magazines were printed and distributed and our German office was instantly on the phone to us because the "whole new *range* of product" had been translated as "a whole new *stove* of product."

## WHEN YOU RELY ON A LOCAL TRANSLATOR

We were not very happy about our first effort in Germany. On the second round we had the agency send the advertisement directly to our German sales manager so he could check the translation. That brought forth a problem of another dimension: the sales manager became an advertising copywriter and elected to rewrite the ad to suit what he thought was necessary in the market. He even added in engineering features not available with our product!

## HOW TO RELY ON DISTRIBUTORS

After many attempts at establishing some uniformity in our advertising, we finally decided the only real solution would be to develop a whole series of ads in various languages, put them in a specially prepared booklet, and tell our customers that any and all advertising could only be authorized if it came from the booklet.

Then we really went crazy and decided it was time to produce a 20-minute film.

## LOCAL SALES MEETINGS NEED A MOVIE

What a wonderful strategy we evolved! Our distributors could assemble their customers at a mini-sales conference, and we would send a film in their language showing the factory, our engineering, our history, and our products. The movie was produced with a minimum amount of on-screen dialogue. Narration was to be used so we could add in different translations, almost at will, to accomplish our goal of a truly international film.

First we tried it in Spanish. Since Spanish takes considerably longer than English, we had to redo major parts of the film to deal with a longer narrative in Spanish. Then we realized there were idiomatic differences among countries in Latin America. Perfectly harmless words in Mexican Spanish had a tendency to become absolutely filthy words in Venezuela or Argentina. The answer was to use a Colombian announcer since the Spanish of Colombia was the "purest" we could find.

A local German radio station produced German voices for us, and the people in Germany decided that those "American Germans" had lost touch with their native tongue.

The film finally went all over the world in English, and most showings were accompanied by a translator standing alongside the screen. While there was concern about the use of English, we discovered that the audiences generally only wanted to see what the factories and facilities of their American product looked like.

## USING A WORLDWIDE ADVERTISING AGENCY

In spite of ourselves, we were doubling sales at a rapid rate and finally decided we could be a client of a truly worldwide agency. Convinced that the philosophy of creating ads was basically the same in each office, we plunged ahead with a clear-cut strategy. The U.S. office would maintain final creative authority for all of our advertising, and we would, of course, have the last approval. The chain of command was from our headquarters down into each area of the world, and it was not to be violated.

If an overseas distributor or one of our own salespeople abroad went into a local office of our agency, we knew about it, and everyone knew the agency would only function on the system we had set up, i.e., no one could change a media schedule or substitute an ad or incur any expense on behalf of our product with any of the agency's offices without first requesting permission from us.

### What About NIH?

Our agency control system worked fine until a European sales manager decided to turn it into a "them or me" contest. He was a very good salesman and a terrible advertising person, but he didn't think so. He screamed long enough and loud enough about our advertising strategies that, sadly, some people began to listen.

In a moment of apparent weakness, we dropped the agency and all its benefits to appease a rampant sales manager. Shortly thereafter, we dropped the sales manager because his behavior became increasingly obnoxious, but it was too late to regain the momentum of the agency's initial efforts, and we found ourselves looking for another agency that could help us capture the success we were winning. If there is a lesson to be learned here, it is simply that you should rely on your intuitive reactions; the first agency was a very classy, serious, and professional company doing outstanding work.

Be careful and be prudent in the decision process when it comes to advertising and sales promotion. Build up copy strategies and media strategies; employ solid research to justify actions you wish to take; and don't be afraid of being what you are, an American company with American products.

## SUMMARY

Your sensitivity to a culture and the way you interact personally with people must also reflect itself in the way you advertise products. This does not mean you have to sterilize your advertising and sales promotion efforts to feel you are conforming to another market, but it does mean you have to understand some subtle differences.

One of the most successful advertisements we ever used in Europe on automotive replacement shock absorbers was a U.S. western theme with a saddle, sheriff's star, and our product Red Ryder, coming out of a saddle holster. While that ad, which had very little copy, probably would have also done well in Japan (where visual illusions are important), we chose to create a special ad for Japan. It was a simple illustration of a four-wheel-drive vehicle in the distance driving over the crest of a hill and a cluster of shock absorbers in the corner of the page.

The worksheets on the following pages will assist you in

establishing the strategy and budget you can operate with when you start on your advertising campaign. Be creative, be a bit adventuresome, and be American—with good taste!

# APPENDIX

## ADVERTISING/SALES PROMOTION STRATEGY AND BUDGET DEVELOPMENT WORKSHEET

In order to create truly effective advertising and sales promotion, globally or country by country, you first need to create an effective strategic plan. This plan is intended to help you focus on issues of significance in building the business. Only you can do it; do not rely on an advertising agency or sales promotion firm since you are the best judge of your products and their benefits to the ultimate buyer. An advertising agency or sales promotion firm can implement your concept after you have given them the strategic plan.

1. *What does each product offer that is unique or special to the buyer?* Think about issues of product engineering and quality, as well as distribution benefits, e.g., high order fill rates, and list them below:

   *a.*

   *b.*

   *c.*

   *d.*

   *e.*

   *Are these really the very best attributes of your product? Do not look yet at cost as a benefit!*
2. *How do the above attributes give you an advantage or even parity with the major competitors?* Are there issues here that are clearly superior to other products? Are you just playing "me too"?
3. Given the market(s) in which you want to promote this product, *what kind of timing do you think is required to insure that your message is being conveyed?*

( ) Will need at least one to 2 months.
( ) Will need 2 to 6 months.
( ) Will need 6 to 9 months.
( ) Will need a sustaining program.

At this point, you have begun to think objectively about the basic issues you will face in advertising and sales promotion, i.e., what it is you *truly* have to sell and *how long it might take to communicate effectively to your market.*

Now let's consider what our options might be:

4. *What is the competition doing to communicate its messages to the same market?* Don't always assume they are doing it better simply because they are already there and/or because they may have a lead on you in terms of market development. Are they using:

   *a.* Trade and/or consumer magazines? Which ones? How often?

   *b.* Point-of-sale pieces, e.g., countertop displays, shelf talkers, or contests?

   *c.* Billboards or outdoor signs? Where?

   *d.* Other things (list them).

5. Of equal importance, *what is the competition saying in their advertising/sales promotion* about their product, their position in the market, their thrust to be a success?

6. Without thinking about refuting the competition's statements, and looking back at question 1, *what can you say that might cause the customer to think twice about the competitor* and reflect a bit on your offering?

7. *What unique features exist with your product* that will cause buyers to think of it as *quality* and as *unique* to an American style of life or business? Think a bit about Timberland shoes, rough-and tumble-shoes, that sell millions of dollars of products in Italy because they represent *us*!

8. Now practice creating a strategic paragraph about what you want to sell; here are some samples of the way you might want to think about this:

Product X offers a special configuration of unique engineering features, including hand-finished valves of specially created alloys. These can offer users a product which provides extended performance over any other product on the market today. To effectively convey this to our market, we believe that in-store displays and window posters, tied with an every-other-month schedule of full-page trade ads extolling these same features can generate sales volume in excess of $000,000,000 by the end of year 2.

You have begun to focus on the real issues of your advertising and sales promotion effort; you have given your advertising/promotion people the nucleus of what you want to communicate, and you have established a goal.

9. *You don't have any features that excell over the competition?* Try a strategy statement like this:

Product X is manufactured in Milwaukee (or Cincinnati or wherever), where the traditions of excellence of our original settlers from Germany (or Sweden or France or China or whatever) have been carried forward to the quality standards we consider a matter of prime importance to our business. Allied with the highest order-fill rates of the industry, we believe we can achieve sales success by the end of year 2 of $000,000,000 using in-store displays, window posters, and an advertising schedule in local trade magazines.

Too often you won't see the forest for the trees, but if you are succeeding here, you will succeed over there—once you stop to think about what makes you a success now!

10. *How do you pay for all this?* That's the easiest part; you are seeking incremental sales by expanding overseas, and that incremental volume will generate advertising and promotion dollars in the following way:

> Let's say you forecast sales in country Z of 10,000 cases or units or whatever form of measurement you wish to use. Let's further assume that you have a gross margin goal of 35 percent. For the sake of clarity, look at a product selling FOB U.S. port

at $25/case; a 35 percent gross means you will gross $8.75/case; on 10,000 cases, that is $87,500 from country Z. If you allocate $2/case for advertising and promotion, your budget for country Z alone will be $20,000, and you will still be earning a 27 percent gross on business you never even had before!

Here's the formula:

*a.* Selling price ______

*b.* Multiplied by percent gross margin = actual gross dollars, minus ______

*c.* Dollars per unit for advertising/promotion ______

*d.* Adjusted gross margin ______

In the above example, you need to watch your sales progress carefully. If the performance of the market appears to show you will exceed your sales target, you can maintain the original budget and watch your gross margin grow. If, on the other hand, you want to remain aggressive, you can build up the budget with the growing volume, maintain your adjusted gross, and watch things grow.

If you begin to see the market falter and, for example, it appears you may only sell 80 percent of your target, you can reduce the budget by 20 percent and sustain the margin you expect.

# CHAPTER 12

# OVERSEAS RESEARCH, INTELLIGENCE, AND NIH

## or "I'VE LIVED HERE ALL MY LIFE, DON'T TELL ME ANYTHING"

One of the major phenomena when you begin to develop an export business is that your overseas agents suddenly assume an aura of irrefutable knowledge not only about their business but also the entire market and all of its subtleties, political or otherwise.

This is a quiet but understandable phenomenon, sometimes defined as the Not Invented Here (NIH) syndrome. In case you have missed becoming aware of it, or need a refresher, the elements are as follow:

1. Most people, in *their* environment, home, office, native country, city of birth, etc. generally feel that *they* are a bit closer to knowing a situation in their environment than anyone else. As a result, they believe that *they* are in a better position than others from the outside to solve a problem of mutual involvement. In other words, this is the "how-do-they-know-as-much-as-I-do" element.
2. Virtually everyone, in various forms, practices what can be characterized as selective reception, perception, and retention. You've seen such people, and they've seen you. We all tend to hear what we want to hear; we interpret it the way we want to; and we remember what we want to remember.

## WHO'S THE CENTER OF THE UNIVERSE?

Curiously, there are very few people with whom you do business who will actually know any more about their market for your goods than you, if you do your homework well. They will surely know about their own business, employment practices, pricing, etc., but they will probably be no better informed than anyone else when it comes to planning, promotion, competitive strategy, and a myriad of other issues vital to your success and theirs.

We all tend to have a proprietary interest in the things we do, and each of us tends to see other things as relative to where we are. (This is the "I'm-the-center-of-the-universe" concept.) An interesting way of describing this was used in asking an audience in Florida where California was. Each person responded simply by saying it was west of Florida. (They were referring to themselves as the focal point to describe where something was.) No one volunteered that it was south of Washington and Oregon or next to Nevada.

If we recognize that there are certain behavioral aspects in each of our lives that tend to impact on others and in our overall decision-making process, what can we do to insure near-perfect information flows and better business decisions?

### When Will NIH Rear Its Ugly Head?

First, begin with a "cause," a substantial business reason to justify doing something in a market, here or overseas. Has a competitor started to expand elsewhere? Is business growth a bit stagnant? Do you need some fresh thinking about a new production or distribution facility? How is your product versus its competition? Have customer attitudes changed about your company or your product? Have your own employees taken on a different attitude?

Any or all of these developments should be symptoms causing you to look at reasons that may handicap your growth. Here is one place where NIH can interfere if you are not careful. As a manager, you have an obligation to find the right solution to problems, but the people you ask may have their own, often hidden, agenda, including a great dose of NIH.

## Getting over the Conflict

The simplest way to avoid an NIH response, either with your suggestions or in asking for these of others, is to retain a neutral third party who has the ability to obtain answers that will tactfully help you. By hiring a neutral person of value for you and your associates, and by letting the neutral party ascertain the issues independent of you or anyone else, you will be in a position to sit down with your overseas colleagues and work together on a common understanding of a problem. Neither side begins with prejudgements on an issue when both sides are reviewing valid research from an outsider.

Thus, there are steps to continue the process and to avoid people feeling they have lost their personal proprietorship. If you retain the services of such local resources as local, but reputable, advertising agencies, promotional firms, production and machine tool designers, etc., they will become agents of change and development—quite separate from the emotionally laden relationship you and your NIH-practicing associates might have.

Sounds easy, but there are plenty of pitfalls:

1. Someone will comment, "I already know what the problem is; I was about to fix it based on the following. . . ."
2. Your overseas manager will add, "My salespeople tell me what the customers think." This actually is the old "they-are-selling-you, you're-not-selling-them" axiom. Everyone tells everybody else what they think the others wants to hear, and that's how each side hopes it will sell its idea.
3. Skeptics will join in, "How do I know I can trust the research findings?" Now you have to teach market research to the skeptics to convince them of its validity.

## How Then Do You Overcome NIH?

Let's look at a number of situations and see how solutions were developed and implemented.

First, let's look at NIH on an organizational level. The international trade division of a Fortune 500 company worked with various business unit managers and assisted them in developing overseas business. Success depended upon the goodwill established between business units and the international people. The international division needed to present itself as organized, efficient, understanding, and capable of success without diminishing each business unit's stature in each manager's mind or the mind of corporate senior management.

Traditionally, everyone in this setup wanted to share in the glory of sales victories, but if things didn't work out perfectly well, a scapegoat was sought. The scapegoat tended to be the international division, and its people's morale and performance suffered as a result. NIH reared its ugly head whenever things weren't perfectly smooth; hence, there was little risk taking by people in the international division and even less reward earning.

## The Use of Independent Researchers

An independent research company conducted a telephone survey of each business unit manager and other key executives in the business units involved with the international division's activities and policy development. Management at the top corporate level was aware of this effort and agreed to the research. But no one else in the firm knew it was being done, much less for whom and for what purpose.

The basic research concept (and you must have a reason when you do research) was to determine what each business unit's perception was of how it conducted business overseas, the value of such business, and the role of the company's international division as each manager perceived it in terms of the business unit's goals.

## What the Data Did to Help

Once the research was in hand to provide a business-unit-by-business unit profile, it became relatively easy to deal with each unit manager in terms of his or her need and desire for success as well as his or her perception of what success should be. In effect, the NIH aspects of each manager became an "open book" allowing the international division to better understand the motivations of the managers, who felt they and they alone really knew their business.

## ANOTHER PROBLEM, ANOTHER SOLUTION

A manufacturing joint venture in Latin America had oversold, overdistributed, and overadvertised its product to a point that no one in the channel of distribution was making any money. The customer was having a wonderful time shopping between outlets, but the manufacturer and his selling partners were at war with each other, fighting for better prices that would make them more competitive than their neighbors.

Marketing efforts of the manufacturer were fragmented by internal differences and a real inability to look objectively at the problem. Anyone with cash could buy an inventory, but because everyone had an inventory, the selling price from factory to reseller kept dropping. All of this activity was necessary to keep the factory producing!

Again, a market research firm was retained as an independent third party to collect data showing the manufacturer that there were solid reasons not to sell to everyone desiring an inventory in the market.

### Should It Be Qualitative or Quantitative?

A quantitative answer in research—an answer based on statistics, numbers, and projections of hard facts—will always support your case better because it is harder to disprove. On the other hand, qualitative, "touchy/feely" research on people's perceptions and feelings may lead you to a lengthier evaluation of the issues and a response based on more creative things.

### Truly Working with NIH

To work with and overcome NIH, and to deal with it because it will always be present in each of us, you must recognize the operating environment before you get in too deep. Knowing that people, including yourself, will want to defend their position, right or wrong, you should always try to collect some degree of data or information which, by its source or nature, is difficult to refute.

Consider the advantage of personal experience and knowledge of your associates. Let everyone participate in the decision-making process, and, most important, consider the long-term value of the relationships you are building with your overseas associates and the value of building the business together as a team before you decide to play the "bull in a China shop."

If business grows and prospers, NIH will begin to diminish in the overall strategic process. But communication is a key factor along with understanding and a keen sense of knowing what is important and necessary to make a decision based on solid evidence.

## One Interesting Research Technique

In Chapter 1 we talked about doing research with Mexican tire dealers concerning their attitudes about a special, private brand of shock absorber. Once you get the responses you want from the audience, what do you do to array the data in a meaningful, understandable fashion so that people can relate to them and respond to your information?

The following page shows a figure labeled "Mexican Tire Dealers, 1982." The information collected from them is diagrammed in such a fashion as to show what that audience was truly thinking about.

First, there was a central opinion, held by virtually every tire dealer, that "a special brand of shock absorbers for tire dealers would be interesting if it met my needs." That central belief told us we were going in the right direction, and further analysis of the qualitative, verbatim comments from the dealers showed us the satellite beliefs held by various segments of the dealer population in support of the overall statement, "if it met my needs."

These satellites included the areas shown with comments such as, "My customers expect prompt service"; "Price would

## MEXICAN TIRE DEALERS, 1982

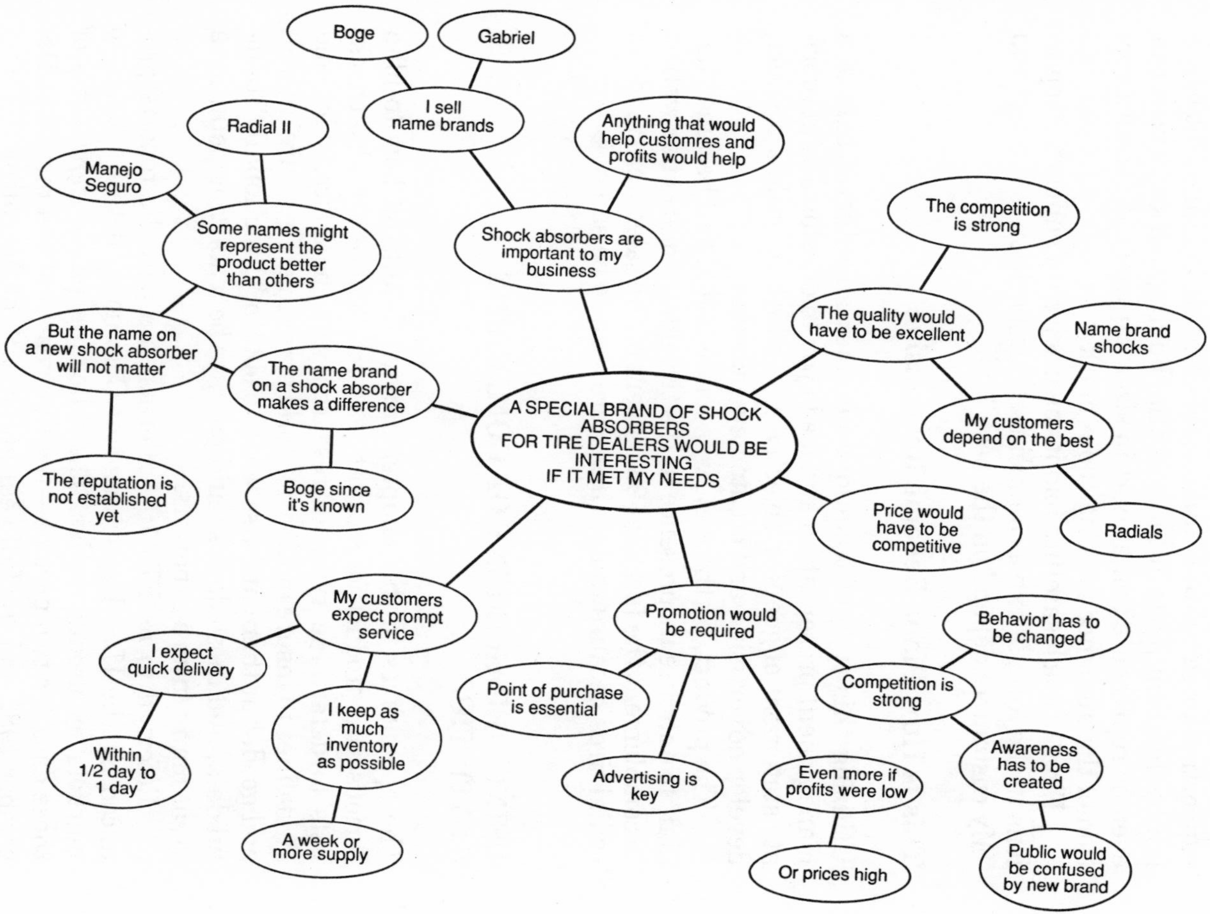

have to be competitive"; "Promotion would be required," and; "The quality would have to be excellent." In all, there are six supporting or satellite opinions representing six different needs felt by different parts of the potential buying market. These can even be represented on a chart in sizes varying with the proportion of the audience making the remark.

Finally, each satellite had its own series of supporting opinions in the form of extra comments: "Competition is strong" and "My customers depend on the best."

### This Is How Plans Become Responsive

Utilizing this type of technique becomes an integral part of a management presentation and leads you to develop an appropriate statement of goals or objectives on which to build a product, develop advertising and create new markets.

The product, by the way, was name-tested and became "Radial" to enhance its presence in the tire dealer market as well as to complement the fact that 98 percent of the sales were made in radial tires because radial tires were seen to be safer.

## USING DEPARTMENT OF COMMERCE STATISTICS

The appendixes to this chapter provide details on how to plan serious and productive market research. There are also checklists to determine types of research you should consider and guidelines to insure quality for solid planning. These are all well and good, but there are also ways to obtain "directionally" helpful data, and these data should perhaps be a starting point for a great many future exporters.

Referred to as FT-410 bulletins, the periodic reports produced by the U.S. Department of Commerce detail exports to markets by product codes. The following pages show some of these data for two periods—the full year and the month of December 1982 and the full year and month of December 1987.

If you are in a business producing lubricants for automobiles, you can look at coded area 5982090, "Lubricating Oil and Grease Additive Mixtures NSPF LB." You will see from the table for 1982 that exports from this country to Argentina went from $8,383,000 in 1982 to $7,618,000 in 1987; you will also see that Brazil is about the same for both periods, and that Japan has dropped from $68,162,000 to $47,609,000.

When you look at the exchange rate table in Chapter 5 and examine the currency rates for 1982–87 for Japan, for example, the yen/dollar ratio has gone in favor of the United States for exports (less yen for each dollar), and the exportation of lubricants has not trended in the same direction. This is something an exporter of lubricating oils would want examine with his or her distributors in Japan and with any other sources of information available.

The Department of Commerce data are not without flaws, but they can be directionally helpful if used prudently as a preliminary planning device.

# APPENDIX A

## HOW TO SERIOUSLY PLAN EFFECTIVE, PRODUCTIVE OVERSEAS RESEARCH

There are myriad ways to collect information on the potentials in a marketplace; some are more expensive than others, some are more thorough, some are a waste of time and money. This worksheet is designed to help you decide (1) if you need research, and (2) how you might wish to conduct the effort.

First, as a warning, be very careful of the information you receive from salespeople in any market, whether they are your employees or your agents! It is human nature for each of us, when pressed, to tell our bosses what we think they want to hear. This system of communication starts at the lowest possible level, and rises to a point where a CEO might as well not listen sometimes.

1. Library Research (existing data centers):
   The U.S. Department of Commerce offers a variety of statistical services to give you directional information in terms of market-by-

## SCHEDULE E COMMODITY BY COUNTRY-DOMESTIC MERCHANDISE-DECEMBER 1982

See "Explanation of Statistics" for information on coverage, definition of f.a.s. export valuation, security restrictions, sampling procedures, sources of error in the data, OTH CTY (other countries), and other definitions and features of the export statistics. The figure preceding Canada is the number in the sample for Canada. "SC" at the end of the alphabetic commodity description identifies "Special Category" commodities. Dash (-) represents zero. Z-Less than one-half of rounded unit)

| Country of destination | Schedule E commodity number, description, and unit of quantity | | | |
|---|---|---|---|---|
| | Current month | | Cumulative, January to date | |
| | Net quantity | Value (000 dollars) | Net quantity | Value (000 dollars) |
| ICELAND | - | - | 11 360 | 205 |
| SWEDEN | 15 558 | 54 | 77 611 | 769 |
| NORWAY | - | - | 26 936 | 682 |
| DENMARK | 93 | 2 | 3 701 | 77 |
| U KING | 36 198 | 420 | 243 994 | 2 983 |
| IRELAND | 5 368 | 51 | 25 123 | 318 |
| NETHLDS | 1 031 | 61 | 187 224 | 1 885 |
| BELGIUM | 10 153 | 141 | 97 480 | 1 159 |
| FRANCE | 2 083 | 46 | 140 620 | 1 011 |
| FR GERM | 14 567 | 175 | 96 739 | 1 747 |
| SWITZLD | 3 591 | 48 | 23 189 | 316 |
| POLAND | 7 925 | 182 | 11 578 | 209 |
| SPAIN | 1 072 | 16 | 27 329 | 404 |
| PORTUGL | 256 | 11 | 3 104 | 64 |
| ITALY | 6 257 | 152 | 113 309 | 1 971 |
| GREECE | 32 | 2 | 17 926 | 292 |
| TURKEY | - | - | 12 146 | 153 |
| LEBANON | 10 233 | 41 | 38 627 | 276 |
| IRAQ | 13 | 1 | 5 332 | 100 |
| ISRAEL | 970 | 21 | 36 053 | 589 |
| JORDAN | 1 472 | 9 | 14 654 | 121 |
| KUWAIT | 81 | 5 | 87 975 | 601 |
| S ARAB | 64 244 | 750 | 459 510 | 5 910 |
| QATAR | 900 | 6 | 4 079 | 72 |
| ARAB EM | 860 | 7 | 97 114 | 1 045 |

| Country of destination | Schedule E commodity number, description, and unit of quantity | | | |
|---|---|---|---|---|
| | Current month | | Cumulative, January to date | |
| | Net quantity | Value (000 dollars) | Net quantity | Value (000 dollars) |
| CHILE | - | - | 149 343 | 186 |
| BRAZIL | 5 550 | 6 | 95 110 | 152 |
| ARGENT | 17 000 | 22 | 166 586 | 200 |
| SWEDEN | 11 269 | 10 | 282 993 | 351 |
| FINLAND | - | - | 109 843 | 138 |
| U KING | 83 540 | 99 | 1 656 398 | 2 064 |
| NETHLDS | 42 069 | 48 | 842 457 | 1 019 |
| BELGUM | 134 985 | 121 | 2 376 222 | 1 650 |
| FRANCE | 22 200 | 25 | 291 150 | 300 |
| FR GERM | 43 257 | 67 | 1 553 194 | 2 145 |
| GERM DR | - | - | 106 688 | 158 |
| SWITZLD | 69 201 | 115 | 729 081 | 919 |
| SPAIN | - | - | 458 728 | 248 |
| ITALY | 80 100 | 36 | 1 646 241 | 940 |
| GREECE | - | - | 149 693 | 159 |
| TURKEY | - | - | 54 849 | 98 |
| IRAQ | - | - | 440 607 | 443 |
| IRAN | - | - | 44 400 | 89 |
| KUWAIT | - | - | 313 656 | 162 |
| S ARAB | 42 151 | 77 | 343 793 | 431 |
| ARAB EM | - | - | 104 300 | 116 |
| BAHRAIN | - | - | 52 948 | 81 |
| THAILND | 4 683 | 6 | 296 397 | 256 |
| MALAYSA | 32 966 | 43 | 303 587 | 467 |
| SINGAPR | 512 964 | 364 | 4 051 890 | 3 482 |

| Country of destination | Schedule E commodity number, description, and unit of quantity | | | |
|---|---|---|---|---|
| | Current month | | Cumulative, January to date | |
| | Net quantity | Value (000 dollars) | Net quantity | Value (000 dollars) |
| 5982090 LUBRICATING OIL AND GREASE ADDITIVE MIXTURES NSPF LB | | | | |
| GUATMAL | - | - | 63 982 | 107 |
| SALVADR | - | - | 138 278 | 191 |
| HONDURA | 77 289 | 58 | 1 148 264 | 1 012 |
| NICARAG | - | - | 1 103 544 | 813 |
| C RICA | 3 403 | 6 | 158 111 | 117 |
| PANAMA | 71 983 | 106 | 1 043 992 | 948 |
| BAHAMAS | - | - | 308 288 | 163 |
| JAMAICA | 1 113 628 | 678 | 2 784 867 | 1 791 |
| DOM REP | 1 098 | 5 | 89 788 | 121 |
| TRINID | 181 653 | 191 | 3 094 742 | 2 574 |
| N ANTIL | 17 630 | 25 | 896 148 | 784 |
| COLOMB | 361 881 | 261 | 9 819 789 | 7 848 |
| VENEZ | 189 593 | 166 | 18 223 476 | 15 371 |
| SURINAM | 2 620 | 5 | 2 608 237 | 554 |
| ECUADOR | 1 170 579 | 922 | 5 948 938 | 4 516 |
| PERU | 191 258 | 148 | 3 495 658 | 2 929 |
| BOLIVIA | - | - | 2 205 575 | 1 733 |
| CHILE | 227 943 | 211 | 6 415 070 | 4 379 |
| BRAZIL | 8 517 898 | 2 927 | 42 142 020 | 26 826 |
| PARAGUA | - | - | 344 755 | 173 |
| URUGUAY | 26 600 | 14 | 480 522 | 481 |
| ARGENT | 1 432 719 | 1 159 | 9 691 042 | 8 383 |
| SWEDEN | 253 724 | 300 | 2 577 314 | 2 253 |

| | | | | |
|---|---|---|---|---|
| OMAN | 1 160 | 12 | 10 950 | 271 |
| BAHRAIN | - | - | 8 467 | 99 |
| INDIA | 2 931 | 31 | 28 370 | 400 |
| PAKISTN | 67 | 4 | 2 470 | 72 |
| THAILND | 1 301 | 20 | 118 919 | 1 217 |
| MALAYSA | 69 | 1 | 16 628 | 142 |
| SINGAPR | 11 381 | 216 | 398 531 | 6 035 |
| INDHSIA | 143 | 3 | 103 893 | 1 441 |
| PHIL R | 2 146 | 25 | 58 974 | 844 |
| KOR REP | 16 421 | 229 | 218 856 | 4 082 |
| HG KONG | 5 952 | 100 | 71 365 | 2 482 |
| CHINA T | 11 148 | 188 | 166 202 | 2 296 |
| JAPAN | 24 093 | 441 | 315 109 | 5 519 |
| AUSTRAL | 2 605 | 51 | 94 834 | 1 606 |
| N ZEAL | 806 | 21 | 15 554 | 231 |
| SO P IS | - | - | 17 325 | 80 |
| FR P IS | 619 | 8 | 9 070 | 90 |
| T PAC I | 25 | 1 | 12 921 | 148 |
| ALGERIA | 886 845 | 1 847 | 903 196 | 1 914 |
| LIBYA | - | - | 17 961 | 168 |
| EGYPT | 2 920 | 35 | 51 946 | 613 |
| CNRY I | - | - | 13 637 | 105 |
| CAMROON | - | - | 2 620 | 67 |
| IVY CST | 259 | 5 | 7 569 | 127 |
| GHANA | 2 685 | 30 | 10 360 | 135 |
| NIGERIA | 1 736 | 18 | 26 937 | 275 |
| ANGOLA | 818 | 10 | 18 514 | 233 |
| O W AF | - | - | 15 389 | 61 |
| REP SAF | 4 390 | 31 | 44 160 | 659 |
| OTH CTY | 4 374 | 53 | 72 797 | 801 |
| TOTAL | 1 800 989 | 8 434 | 13 457 893 | 102 812 |

5982050 FUEL OIL ADDITIVE PREPARATIONS, NSPF LB

| | | | | |
|---|---|---|---|---|
| CANADA | 375 839 | 381 | 2 306 247 | 3 020 |
| MEXICO | - | - | 133 839 | 83 |
| PANAMA | 905 | 2 | 95 133 | 118 |
| JAMAICA | 62 800 | 75 | 582 889 | 690 |
| DOM REP | - | - | 52 416 | 65 |
| PHIL R | 44 199 | 25 | 845 018 | 1 159 |
| KOR REP | 33 307 | 48 | 362 413 | 336 |
| HG KONG | - | - | 208 439 | 124 |
| CHINA T | 9 510 | 16 | 249 822 | 252 |
| JAPAN | 2 756 | 11 | 1 547 699 | 2 225 |
| AUSTRAL | 9 183 | 8 | 434 569 | 593 |
| N ZEAL | - | - | 63 855 | 69 |
| REP SAF | 479 373 | 471 | 1 039 915 | 1 056 |
| OTH CTY | 54 753 | 60 | 613 155 | 700 |
| TOTAL | 2 379 857 | 2 224 | 28 538 080 | 28 546 |

5982085 ANTIKNOCK PREPARATIONS, N.S.P.F. LB

| | | | | |
|---|---|---|---|---|
| CANADA | 374 840 | 907 | 3 677 459 | 8 327 |
| MEXICO | 10 627 | 16 | 139 390 | 250 |
| GUATMAL | - | - | 68 508 | 83 |
| BELIZE | - | - | 333 859 | 256 |
| PANAMA | 68 316 | 31 | 421 037 | 273 |
| BAHAMAS | 120 797 | 84 | 871 240 | 497 |
| BARBADO | 12 302 | 9 | 250 729 | 147 |
| COLOMB | - | - | 176 765 | 80 |
| VENEZ | 7 309 | 4 | 104 278 | 143 |
| ECUADOR | - | - | 366 370 | 703 |
| BRAZIL | - | - | 349 839 | 316 |
| U KING | - | - | 36 154 | 146 |
| NETHLDS | 918 | 4 | 276 770 | 601 |
| FRANCE | 4 867 | 4 | 42 934 | 130 |
| FR GERM | 386 | 1 | 202 699 | 311 |
| SWITZLD | 8 012 | 11 | 42 614 | 82 |
| SPAIN | - | - | 558 857 | 501 |
| ISRAEL | 257 040 | 190 | 259 332 | 202 |
| S ARAB | 11 043 | 18 | 56 234 | 121 |
| INDIA | - | - | 128 527 | 112 |
| PHIL R | - | - | 77 976 | 125 |
| KOR REP | 4 800 | 4 | 64 929 | 73 |
| JAPAN | 1 457 | 2 | 49 637 | 369 |
| AUSTRAL | - | - | 68 164 | 124 |
| OTH CTY | 69 737 | 53 | 443 193 | 614 |
| TOTAL | 952 451 | 1 336 | 9 087 494 | 14 585 |
| NORWAY | 17 450 | 20 | 134 733 | 108 |
| FINLAND | - | - | 855 130 | 821 |
| DENMARK | 11 510 | 18 | 407 435 | 595 |
| U KING | 213 293 | 220 | 15 585 810 | 13 037 |
| POLAND | - | - | 78 010 | 117 |
| NETHLDS | 926 700 | 672 | 62 072 313 | 32 539 |
| BELGIUM | 4 308 101 | 2 363 | 56 314 199 | 34 268 |
| FRANC | 2 004 974 | 1 326 | 27 017 876 | 22 639 |
| FR GERM | 503 551 | 459 | 4 634 865 | 5 195 |
| AUSTRIA | 5 040 | 9 | 111 910 | 119 |
| SWITZLD | 11 246 | 9 | 440 007 | 622 |
| SPAIN | 532 740 | 591 | 21 648 483 | 13 067 |
| PORTUGL | 9 400 | 9 | 143 809 | 161 |
| ITALY | 605 949 | 534 | 4 573 806 | 4 604 |
| YUGOSLV | - | - | 588 750 | 386 |
| GREECE | - | - | 358 606 | 512 |
| TURKEY | - | - | 889 301 | 630 |
| SYRIA | - | - | 409 290 | 227 |
| LEBANON | 9 | 1 | 584 594 | 500 |
| IRAN | - | - | 4 137 | 71 |
| ISRAEL | 4 481 | 5 | 271 611 | 232 |
| JORDAN | - | - | 92 163 | 65 |
| KUWAIT | 5 500 | 6 | 215 304 | 143 |
| S ARAB | 3 655 866 | 2 493 | 19 291 506 | 14 296 |
| ARAB EM | 106 038 | 101 | 5 406 862 | 4 885 |
| AFGHAN | - | - | 196 746 | 148 |
| INDIA | 1 379 094 | 790 | 18 139 438 | 8 625 |
| PAKISTN | 44 840 | 29 | 2 574 247 | 2 240 |
| BNGLDSH | - | - | 419 871 | 378 |
| SRI LKA | 8 814 | 6 | 596 530 | 485 |
| BURMA | - | - | 222 349 | 281 |
| THAILND | 138 404 | 126 | 4 087 249 | 3 135 |
| MALAYSA | 19 045 | 26 | 618 956 | 838 |
| SINGAPR | 6 684 087 | 4 573 | 77 155 798 | 48 579 |
| INDNSIA | 46 900 | 56 | 2 328 816 | 3 408 |
| PHIL R | 2 029 252 | 1 463 | 12 855 878 | 10 109 |
| CHINA M | - | - | 124 376 | 121 |
| KOR REP | 239 670 | 265 | 10 611 966 | 8 761 |
| JAPAN | 10 095 792 | 6 881 | 93 309 358 | 68 162 |

source: U.S. Department of Commerce, Bulletin FT-410.

# SCHEDULE E COMMODITY BY COUNTRY-DOMESTIC MERCHANDISE-DECEMBER 1987

See "Explanation of Statistics" for information on coverage, definition of f.a.s. export valuation, security restrictions, sampling procedures, sources of error in the data, OTH CTY (other countries), and other definitions and features of the export statistics. The figure preceding Canada is the number in the sample for Canada. "SC" at the end of the alphabetic commodity description identifies "Special Category" commodities. Dash (-) represents zero. Z-Less than one-half of rounded unit)

| Country of destination | Schedule E commodity number, description, and unit of quantity | | | |
|---|---|---|---|---|
| | Current month | | Cumulative, January to date | |
| | Net quantity | Value (000 dollars) | Net quantity | Value (000 dollars) |
| 5982050 FUEL OIL ADDITIVE PREPARATIONS, NSPF LB | | | | |
| CANADA | 627 835 | 354 | 2 461 639 | 2 417 |
| MEXICO | - | - | 296 818 | 195 |
| JAMAICA | 40 700 | 54 | 334 937 | 536 |
| TRINID | 78 580 | 60 | 505 671 | 380 |
| COLOMB | - | - | 76 455 | 97 |
| VENEZ | 1 008 592 | 470 | 5 371 958 | 2 532 |
| SURINAM | - | - | 71 390 | 63 |
| CHILE | 24 946 | 40 | 155 331 | 226 |
| BRAZIL | 16 693 | 53 | 248 407 | 418 |
| ARGENT | 18 000 | 14 | 150 855 | 142 |
| SWEDEN | 57 590 | 219 | 289 684 | 590 |
| FINLAND | - | - | 280 484 | 220 |
| DENMARK | - | - | 30 870 | 74 |
| U KING | 19 458 | 48 | 1 054 179 | 1 196 |
| BELGIUM | 788 396 | 409 | 11 334 440 | 5 575 |
| FRANCE | 38 975 | 51 | 4 520 540 | 4 235 |
| FR GERM | 32 160 | 63 | 435 835 | 610 |
| SPAIN | - | - | 47 347 | 71 |
| ITALY | 68 313 | 104 | 461 819 | 430 |
| KUWAIT | 32 300 | 79 | 112 944 | 195 |
| S ARAB | - | - | 774 085 | 942 |
| INDIA | 31 196 | 50 | 1 195 627 | 646 |
| THAILND | - | - | 401 764 | 484 |
| MALAYSA | 97 486 | 134 | 235 259 | 316 |
| REP SAF | 102 000 | 56 | 248 050 | 132 |
| OTH CTY | 30 396 | 52 | 602 666 | 623 |
| TOTAL | 805 917 | 1 589 | 9 272 800 | 19 915 |
| 5982090 LUBRICATING OIL AND GREASE ADDITIVE MISTURES NSPF LB | | | | |
| CANADA | 6 370 623 | 4 299 | 62 494 971 | 49 536 |
| MEXICO | 7 964 482 | 2 207 | 82 141 519 | 21 917 |
| GUATMAL | 38 124 | 34 | 251 744 | 200 |
| SALVADR | 90 | 6 | 753 564 | 610 |
| HONDURA | 9 939 | 12 | 1 088 156 | 744 |
| C RICA | 14 114 | 24 | 196 955 | 162 |
| PANAMA | 22 086 | 30 | 1 751 129 | 1 169 |
| BERMUDA | 59 210 | 11 | 885 905 | 142 |
| BAHAMAS | 365 160 | 36 | 523 588 | 67 |
| JAMAICA | 269 095 | 165 | 3 215 037 | 1 982 |
| DOM REP | 14 769 | 105 | 919 890 | 1 223 |
| LW WW I | - | - | 145 685 | 101 |
| TRIND | 181 054 | 160 | 785 546 | 639 |
| COLOMB | 569 062 | 432 | 15 455 253 | 8 102 |
| VENEZ | 3 151 784 | 2 370 | 46 382 170 | 33 263 |
| ECUADOR | 824 927 | 447 | 5 492 921 | 3 511 |
| PERU | 971 334 | 522 | 6 354 282 | 3 931 |
| CHILE | 1 329 967 | 801 | 7 712 507 | 5 351 |
| BRAZIL | 4 215 044 | 2 589 | 40 429 397 | 24 287 |
| OTH CTY | 2 953 | 5 | 725 376 | 529 |
| TOTAL | 78 723 054 | 45 949 | 881 943 313 | 514 538 |
| 5988030 HYDRAULIC BRAKE FLUID PREPARATIONS LB | | | | |
| CANADA | 118 500 | 63 | 2 531 902 | 1 214 |
| SALVADR | - | - | 392 972 | 326 |
| HONDURA | - | - | 198 653 | 120 |
| PANAMA | 30 600 | 15 | 234 386 | 140 |
| HAITI | - | - | 97 564 | 122 |
| DOM REP | 40 981 | 35 | 311 511 | 188 |
| ECUADOR | 33 135 | 30 | 1 055 696 | 946 |
| BOLIVIA | - | - | 261 041 | 263 |
| CHILE | 60 969 | 55 | 707 956 | 611 |
| URUGUAY | - | - | 131 070 | 61 |
| ARGENT | - | - | 34 676 | 66 |
| BELGIUM | 960 | 2 | 1 708 977 | 574 |
| FR GERM | - | - | 86 067 | 278 |
| LEBANON | 30 717 | 25 | 225 008 | 195 |
| ISRAEL | - | - | 58 066 | 83 |
| KUWAIT | 55 566 | 58 | 129 997 | 136 |
| S ARAB | 387 379 | 339 | 2 391 519 | 1 968 |
| QATAR | 27 783 | 29 | 89 349 | 91 |
| AFGHAN | - | - | 196 433 | 191 |
| PAKISTN | - | - | 747 721 | 592 |
| SRI LKA | - | - | 305 920 | 116 |

| | | | | |
|---|---|---|---|---|
| SINGAPR | 4 800 | 20 | 812 257 | 580 |
| INDNSIA | - | - | 258 947 | 101 |
| PHIL R | - | - | 179 499 | 228 |
| CHINA M | - | - | 94 872 | 307 |
| KOR REP | - | - | 154 758 | 220 |
| HG KONG | - | - | 645 472 | 533 |
| CHINA T | 22 626 | 48 | 146 582 | 206 |
| JAPAN | 203 161 | 343 | 2 993 533 | 4 985 |
| AUSTRAL | 37 646 | 50 | 1 884 937 | 2 023 |
| N ZEAL | 33 450 | 67 | 476 700 | 683 |
| EGYPT | - | - | 138 900 | 95 |
| REP SAF | - | - | 1 276 161 | 2 348 |
| OTH CTY | 26 847 | 26 | 533 465 | 607 |
| TOTAL | 3 309 750 | 2 756 | 40 444 421 | 35 506 |

5982085 ANTIKNOCK PREPARATIONS, N.S.P.F. LB

| | | | | |
|---|---|---|---|---|
| CANADA | 286 472 | 951 | 2 942 177 | 10 298 |
| MEXICO | 66 665 | 85 | 545 402 | 650 |
| PANAMA | - | - | 143 686 | 125 |
| BERMUDA | 12 904 | 9 | 70 631 | 76 |
| DOM REP | - | - | 103 865 | 66 |
| LW WW I | 15 002 | 22 | 53 182 | 96 |
| TRINID | 10 189 | 6 | 137 807 | 137 |
| N ANTIL | 26 473 | 12 | 265 132 | 220 |
| COLOMB | 7 110 | 14 | 135 003 | 272 |
| VENEZ | 60 | 2 | 671 721 | 1 126 |
| PERU | - | - | 46 555 | 77 |
| CHILE | 4 132 | 6 | 59 698 | 81 |
| U KING | 3 302 | 5 | 456 742 | 1 247 |
| NETHLDS | - | - | 28 851 | 72 |
| BELGIUM | 2 638 | 4 | 86 482 | 142 |
| FRANCE | - | - | 91 276 | 133 |
| FR GERM | 22 159 | 32 | 422 295 | 595 |
| SWITZLD | 4 024 | 6 | 145 957 | 207 |
| ITALY | 1 556 | 9 | 360 659 | 403 |
| ISRAEL | - | - | 70 981 | 145 |
| S ARAB | - | - | 113 871 | 130 |
| MALAYSA | 4 810 | 10 | 44 645 | 71 |
| PHIL R | 2 911 | 6 | 32 743 | 78 |
| CHINA M | 10 784 | 15 | 30 490 | 80 |
| PARAGUA | - | - | 83 836 | 111 |
| URUGUAY | 6 213 | 11 | 355 318 | 409 |
| ARGENT | 517 231 | 509 | 7 404 195 | 7 618 |
| ICELAND | - | - | 88 567 | 184 |
| SWEDEN | 78 010 | 88 | 1 287 856 | 939 |
| NORWAY | 1 850 | 2 | 91 653 | 80 |
| FINLAND | 611 521 | 295 | 14 537 526 | 3 032 |
| U KING | 2 124 354 | 1 806 | 23 866 194 | 18 103 |
| NETHLDS | 3 759 967 | 1 794 | 34 148 441 | 19 199 |
| BELGIUM | 11 646 432 | 5 578 | 125 561 587 | 65 225 |
| FRANCE | 6 429 431 | 3 711 | 45 185 371 | 28 241 |
| FR GERM | 419 645 | 409 | 4 936 426 | 3 826 |
| SWITZLD | - | - | 498 307 | 473 |
| SPAIN | 541 880 | 756 | 3 302 629 | 3 217 |
| ITALY | 163 101 | 168 | 2 732 488 | 2 227 |
| YUGOSLV | - | - | 104 744 | 78 |
| GREECE | 7 333 | 10 | 124 424 | 113 |
| SYRIA | - | - | 106 617 | 145 |
| IRAQ | 647 537 | 673 | 648 975 | 675 |
| ISRAEL | 144 579 | 149 | 207 946 | 276 |
| JORDAN | 10 500 | 7 | 1 101 052 | 721 |
| KUWAIT | - | - | 418 677 | 138 |
| S ARAB | 528 809 | 464 | 4 663 518 | 3 399 |
| ARAB EM | 218 353 | 213 | 2 413 429 | 1 710 |
| INDIA | 1 065 250 | 606 | 13 514 639 | 9 619 |
| PAKISTN | 1 016 980 | 475 | 4 909 086 | 2 903 |
| SRI LKA | 3 776 | 6 | 69 528 | 66 |
| THAILND | 58 336 | 55 | 1 722 350 | 1 582 |
| MALAYSA | 6 380 | 9 | 392 111 | 490 |
| SINGAPR | 7 825 601 | 4 511 | 138 320 582 | 70 101 |
| INDNSIA | 695 343 | 290 | 6 711 137 | 3 101 |
| PHIL R | 701 355 | 559 | 12 367 320 | 6 052 |
| CHINA M | 574 542 | 322 | 3 138 205 | 2 096 |
| KOR REP | 477 211 | 380 | 7 237 919 | 5 976 |
| HG KONG | 230 494 | 207 | 3 403 340 | 2 851 |
| CHINA T | 1 051 179 | 668 | 11 392 048 | 6 312 |
| JAPAN | 6 053 528 | 4 119 | 70 758 263 | 47 609 |
| AUSTRAL | 721 985 | 1 004 | 23 848 541 | 16 750 |
| N ZEAL | 119 220 | 154 | 1 902 476 | 1 980 |
| EGYPT | 1 333 000 | 543 | 3 477 347 | 1 816 |
| SUDAN | - | - | 486 768 | 334 |
| THAILND | - | - | 670 186 | 268 |
| CHINA T | - | - | 127 905 | 101 |
| JAPAN | - | - | 442 562 | 225 |
| EGYPT | 32 882 | 23 | 92 634 | 73 |
| NIGERIA | - | - | 137 906 | 113 |
| ZAMBIA | - | - | 36 504 | 175 |
| OTH CTY | 66 490 | 62 | 969 745 | 591 |
| TOTAL | 885 962 | 737 | 14 373 926 | 9 929 |

5988035 HYDRAULIC TRANSMISSION FLUID PREPARATIONS LB

| | | | | |
|---|---|---|---|---|
| CANADA | 9 110 | 143 | 441 271 | 1 710 |
| MEXICO | 53 032 | 32 | 481 364 | 951 |
| DOM REP | 24 500 | 25 | 45 866 | 68 |
| COLOMB | - | - | 80 188 | 244 |
| VENEZ | - | - | 54 684 | 86 |
| BRAZIL | 232 423 | 229 | 325 484 | 354 |
| U KING | - | - | 155 432 | 461 |
| NETHLDS | 222 822 | 332 | 1 264 706 | 3 043 |
| BELGIUM | 170 870 | 636 | 1 139 873 | 4 456 |
| FRANCE | 35 844 | 44 | 925 992 | 973 |
| SPAIN | - | - | 40 000 | 163 |
| GREECE | - | - | 209 723 | 290 |
| KUWAIT | 72 000 | 16 | 854 543 | 195 |
| S ARAB | 174 | 3 | 194 529 | 91 |
| INDIA | 6 342 | 20 | 45 170 | 139 |
| PAKISTN | - | - | 148 173 | 315 |
| THAILND | - | - | 16 480 | 66 |
| SINGAPR | 26 400 | 107 | 140 710 | 519 |
| CHINA M | - | - | 230 769 | 162 |
| KOR REP | 340 488 | 1 491 | 936 260 | 3 366 |
| HG KONG | 34 707 | 117 | 485 200 | 751 |
| CHINA T | 60 169 | 105 | 272 419 | 340 |
| JAPAN | 9 531 | 18 | 200 683 | 574 |
| AUSTRAL | 27 376 | 82 | 617 318 | 733 |
| N ZEAL | - | - | 43 454 | 69 |
| ALGERIA | - | - | 34 360 | 125 |
| EGYPT | - | - | 32 212 | 82 |
| REP SAF | - | - | 130 752 | 532 |
| OTH CTY | 72 111 | 30 | 902 545 | 509 |
| TOTAL | 1 397 899 | 3 429 | 10 329 960 | 21 369 |

source: U.S. Department of Commerce, Bulletin FT-410.

market potential. As an example, their FT-410 bulletin (see the table on pages 112–115) will show you export values of various items by SIC code into individual countries. While these data can be directionally helpful, some people feel the numbers are not always as correct as they should be, e.g., items coming from Thailand to Canada by way of Oregon might appear as U.S. exports to Canada.

While district offices of the Department of Commerce can provide volumes of data and information, another resource is their Washington D.C. desk officer system. If you want to learn something about the market for widgets in Hong Kong, for example, you would call Nancy Chen at (202) 377–2462. The person for Madagascar is Simon Bensimon at (202) 377–0357, and there are desk officers for every country from Afghanistan to Zimbabwe.

Several years ago I had to learn everything possible about free-standing automotive service centers in Europe. We were looking at the possibility of developing the same concept with a European automobile manufacturer, and two companies had already established themselves in the marketplace.

With the assistance of a Department of Commerce desk officer for Germany and another for Great Britain, I was put in touch with a commercial representative in our embassy in London and another in Hamburg. The London man arranged for me to have an interview with the founder of one of the existing companies, including a serious examination of their income statements and balance sheets; the Hamburg man provided a list of locations, and I was able to rent a car with a driver to visit every location with which we would ultimately compete.

Another supersource of existing data can be found in World Trade Centers. The World Trade Center Association (WTCA) has been in existence over 20 years all over the world. In 55 different countries and in over 160 cities within these countries, WTCA works to bring together different groups of buyers, sellers, and traders to sponsor international trade.

Through the WTCA network, you can gain immediate computer access to worldwide offers to sell and buy. A recent printout showed the following offers to buy around the world: ethyl alcohol, used outboard marine engines, American toys, jogging suits, home alarm systems, air and liquid filters, industrial greases, apple juice concentrate, car batteries, etc.

The headquarters office of the WTCA is in Tower One of the World Trade Center in New York City, (212) 313–4600, and that's where you ought to start. The association also has offices in this country in places as far-flung as Cedar Rapids, Iowa; Las Vegas, Nevada; Oxnard, California; and Portland, Oregon. You need to look in your local phone book too.

Overseas, the WTCA support system can provide you with local introductions all over the Caribbean, in six Latin American countries, in six African countries, virtually everywhere in Europe, in the Middle East, India, and Pakistan, and all over the Far East plus Australia.

2. Customized, market-by-market research:
This can be very serious stuff, involving some real expenditures in dollars, time, and effort. Thus, the first thing you have to think about is simply, "What is it that we want to learn?"

One of the business building situations discussed in this book involved Mexico and a study of the distribution systems for an automotive product, shock absorbers. We wanted to learn what was happening in the traditional distribution system to cause our sales to fall off. Library research in the form of statistical data could not give us the answer, and it was absolutely necessary to send a qualified and objective research team into the field to find an unbiased, nonemotional answer to this question.

A field study in five different German cities was organized and developed because we needed to learn what the trade's perception was of our product versus other products if we wanted to effectively promote the sale of our product. Five different markets in Argentina were researched because we had to find out what the ultimate reason was for consumers to accept one product versus another and what the impact was of something being the same as "original equipment."

When our Mexican company wanted to make a substantial investment to install a tube mill, we had to find out the capacity of the market to absorb more tube production.

In every case of customized research, you must be sure you have a reason to learn something so important it will justify the cost, the effort, and will give you reason to act in a major way when the data is collected. How do you do it?

- *Field surveys.* Your researcher can prepare a questionnaire with you and organize teams of people to go into the field asking questions of the audience that are important to your decision-making process.

  In a very qualitative sense, you can obtain responses that might be arrayed in what is referred to as a "belief dynamics" configuration (see Figure 12–1, Mexican Tire

Dealers-1982). An overall core belief may exist generally within the population you are talking to, but there might be subsets of secondary beliefs. For example, the marketplace may tell the researchers that your widgets are important and exciting (core belief). But one subset may feel their country has a better design; another group may feel your price is too high; a third may believe that delivery is too difficult.

Now you can act with the knowledge that, while you have an important product, various groups within the buying population have to be informed that the design is comparable or better to what they buy; that a higher price may be justified because of greater quality; and you may want to talk to your distributor about increasing inventories to raise order-fill rates.

- *Telephone surveys.* When the market you wish to talk to is small enough, as was the case with the potential customers for a new Mexican tube mill, you can arrange for research to be conducted with a questionnaire administered through a phone call to a sample of those people.

  A good research company will know how to obtain this sort of data in a short phone call. Depending upon the country and your ability to find good researchers there, you might even want to conduct the calls from here if you can resolve the language problem.
- *Mail surveys.* Trying to collect data overseas by mail is extremely difficult unless everything is coordinated in the country where you want the information.

  You and your researcher will have to find a way to make the respondent answer the questionnaire and return it with the least amount of trouble. Remember that our postage stamps won't work on return envelopes in other countries!
- *Warranty cards.* An often overlooked way to collect data, even abroad, is through a well-planned warranty card return system. If you ask the right questions based on what you want and need to know, and if you can arrange for warranty card collection within the country of sale, your distributors can then forward these to you for tabulation and analysis of the data.

  This may well be the least expensive way of collecting information.

In every case of custom research, you need to work with a professional research firm. Do not try to write your own questionnaires unless you are trained how not to create biased or low "no response" returns from your audience.

# APPENDIX B

## MARKET RESEARCH AS AN INFORMATION SYSTEM: A CHECKLIST ON TYPES OF RESEARCH TO BE CONSIDERED

1. Product area:
   The most specific research you can organize would clearly deal with the actual product you have to sell (and/or your competitor's product since there is no reason why you can't learn as much as possible about your competition).

   - *Product acceptance/potential.* This type of research, handled in myriad ways, e.g., focus groups or in-store testing, can be directionally valuable in assisting you toward a decision to introduce or not to introduce a product in any given market. While the real test is actually putting the product out for sale, product acceptance/potential testing can at least give you some directional assistance, and it will surely warn you if you have a real loser.
   - *Competitor acceptance/potential.* Side-by-side comparison studies with consumers, engineers, and anyone relevant to the ultimate buying decision will benefit your product introduction. Testing acceptance levels of competitive products without the presence of your product will offer you an unbiased viewpoint on the item(s) against which you will be waging a sales war. Again, focus groups of 10 to 12 people in a room, led by a trained researcher, will supply you tremendous insights, as will various in-store techniques.
   - *Existing product line.* We all become a bit complacent with our products after a while, especially if we are having any degree of success. Constant improvements in quality, performance, and appearance can lengthen a product's life cycle and help keep its immunity from competitive inroads.

- *Design/characteristics.* The stories of business success and failure due to slight differences in design are famous. For example, woodworking tools in Europe require different handles, even different saw configurations. Thus, the pre-testing of design in prototypes can save millions in failure later on.

2. Business economics/corporate statistics:
Because the world doesn't revolve solely on the decisions made from qualitative types of research, quantitative data can be extremely valuable in the decision-making process and should never be ignored.

    - *Short-and long-range forecasts.* The inputs from industry sources, sales reports, financial services, etc. can be vitally important in your ability to judge the anticipated volume of the business you wish to achieve in a given country. Your advertising/promotion budget process can flow from this sort of information if you allocate dollars on units to be sold.
    - *Business trends.* The world is always in a state of flux; automotive exhaust systems are rapidly being produced in stainless steel, thus greatly reducing the replacement rate for mufflers in the future. Why should people buy a muffler business for the long run? Throwaway products seem to abound in this country, but Europe is more aware of its lack of space for waste disposal. Thus this may be a trend that differs, from country to country.
    - *Pricing analyses.* Export selling can be a market-by-market pricing situation, depending upon the scope of local competition in any given market. Some U.S. prices are based on industry standards that have no bearing overseas, and solid price analyses on a continuum will always be a worthwhile endeavor.
    - *Location studies.* Pedestrian and automotive traffic patterns do indeed differ by country, even by time of day. If your business requires any real estate, you don't want to be in the wrong place at the wrong time simply because you took American standards and transferred them abroad.
    - *Acquisition studies.* Such studies are always worthwhile, even if done only to keep up with the pulse of a

market. Acquisitions have become a significant factor for Americans in dealing with the EEC. Arvin, an automotive parts manufacturer, recently purchased a shock absorber plant in Spain—a solid investment since that plant supplies original equipment products to Ford of Germany. The acquisition of a plant in France or Britain, for example, might not have been as good an idea.

- *Distribution studies.* The patterns and techniques of distribution for various products differ greatly in many countries, especially in Japan. Ample data should be available to outline and understand the differences in distribution for countries and products before you plunge into a market.

3. Sales:
Thanks to the reams of data produced by various organizations, institutes, and associations around the world, as well as by the U.S. Department of Commerce, the opportunities to do various types of sales analysis are available and necessary.

- *Market potential.* Statistical data—a topic discussed earlier—can provide you with directional assistance in terms of understanding a market's ability to provide buyers for your product. Local distributors, chambers of commerce, and embassy personnel all can supply you with data sources.
- *Share analysis.* Much has been written about market share, and there are still some companies who feel share is everything. While you can easily determine market share by comparing available statistics on a market-by-market basis, you should also consider the relative cost of buying additional share points versus the profit level on which you currently operate.
- *Market characteristics.* Government agencies exist, it seems, solely to provide data on their populations, but these reports can be helpful in preliminarily establishing goals or baselines in terms of ideal buyers, their level of existence in a market, etc.
- *Sales analysis.* Over time you will generate your own history of performance, and over time you will be able to evaluate whether or not these numbers represent the type of goal achievement you desire.

- *Promotional evaluations.* The fastest way to achieve sales is through promotional programs since they bring the incentive right into the market in a very direct way. The first trip promotion I established in Australia ("Buy X dollars over X period and earn a trip to Fiji") was quickly measurable. It was then followed up by a second trip promotion (to Hawaii) because the first promotion was so successful and, the numbers of winners was apparent quickly.

### CAVEAT

Don't think that any one of the above research suggestions will be sufficient to guide you successfully into or through a market. You should always think about conducting various types of research—both qualitative and quantitative—and you should make sure that some of the statistical studies become an integral part of your overall and continuing operating system.

# APPENDIX C

## EFFECTIVE RESEARCH REQUIRES EFFECTIVE PLANNING: A CHECKLIST TO SEE IF IT'S GOOD RESEARCH

The development and utilization of truly good research is absolutely essential in any decision-making process unless you are obsessed with believing in coin tosses and rabbit's feet above all else.

1. *You must practice proven data collection techniques; you must formulate the hypothesis you wish to test before you begin the project; and you must pretest everything!*

   This sounds very academic, but it shouldn't. There are proven ways of collecting information, whether through field surveys or government statistical reports. You shouldn't look for such typical short cuts as asking sales people exclusively, sitting around a bar at night with customers, star gazing. They don't work!

Further, you absolutely have to know what you are seeking when you collect any data. Do you want to know the effects of a promotion or a competitor's promotion? Do you want to know the impact on your customers of a proposed new product variation?

Finally, you must test the research technique before you rely on it. Is the data source valid and continuous? Were the questions prejudicial in any way? Did people truly understand what it was they were being asked? Did your marketing person correctly tabulate the indexes he was developing?

2. *Don't be afraid to innovate to find solutions to a problem.*

After jumping up and down about procedure, I'm now telling you to innovate. Is that consistent? It is if you do it with intelligence. Simply because no one has ever done a door-to-door survey in a market, there is no reason for you not to consider it unless the people in that market simply will not greet anyone at their doorway!

I once worked with a bunch of people who air-expressed fresh-cut fruit all over the country to test a new product consisting of fresh fruit. In case of delay, they also included a color photograph of the fresh-fruit product, but being innovative meant allowing potential customers to see the actual product in its prototype state rather than as a picture.

3. *Try to use techniques which are truly applicable to the situation and your needs at the time.*

I've talked about numerous ways to collect data, but some are always more appropriate than others. Focus groups are good barometers for a small group of people's feelings about a concept, but they would kill your budget if you wanted to use them to test brand awareness versus competitive products in a multiproduct environment: there would simply be too much to talk about in a couple of hours, and you would never be sure you had collected reasonable responses.

Don't hesitate to let your research firm send people out into the field to collect data if it is the appropriate way to get the right information. Don't use mail or the phone when you want to get detailed, qualitative information or need to explain and/or show someone something.

4. *Always define well the issue to be questioned.*

This sounds familiar, and it should because research will cost you a lot of money, and you should always be sure you need the research, are willing to pay to have it done well, and have a well-defined issue to be covered and resolved. Remember, too, that you may not like the answers!

5. *The research you buy will be valuable to you only if you feel you got what you paid for!*

   Spend as much time as you or your marketing personnel can with the research facility you plan to use. Don't let anyone begin to do anything until you are comfortable with what's to be done and until you can truly understand what is being done and why!

6. *Review and present the findings with a course of action.*

   When you can do this, you have accomplished everything you set out to do with the research, provided your course of action is at least, in part, a result of the data reported.

# CHAPTER 13

# ENJOY YOUR VISITS OVERSEAS

## or "YOU MAY NOT NEED A SWIMSUIT AT THE SAUNA"

A great many people overseas are very eager to show us some of the relatively unique and interesting aspects of their lives. The way they live and the things they do for recreation and pleasure can often be very different from the things we are accustomed to in the United States. Sadly, too many people tend to become introverted or even chauvinistic when it comes to trying something new or different, and we may thus lose an opportunity to develop a relationship abroad that often can transcend a written contract in solving business issues.

While we probably tend to withdraw from a fear of the unknown, we may, in fact, be telling those who want to share some part of their culture with us that we don't want their values or customs. How sad when there is so much to learn in this world, and when simple acts of interest and friendship can do so much to help!

### SIGNS/SYMBOLS WITH DIFFERENT MEANINGS

When you hear stories about great mistakes in courtesy, our tendency is to steer clear of situations that may be loaded with the possibility of a mistake. I've been told that Winston Churchill's famous V for victory sign can even be a problem in Great Britain. If you do it with your palm facing out, it's supposed to be the same as giving someone "the finger." How sad! We have all heard about not showing the bottom of your shoe to an Arab, not being too demonstrative in Scandinavia, and taking off your shoes before entering some rooms in Japan. What else can there be?

- If someone in Colombia circles his fingers in the OK sign, and then puts them over his nose, it means a person in question is homosexual.
- While a head tap in some Latin American countries means "thinking," elsewhere it might mean "crazy."
- The Texas A&M longhorn sign with your hands, first and last finger up, is a sign of good luck in Brazil.
- Don't snap your fingers in France or Belgium; it might be interpreted as something vulgar.
- Thumbs up is OK in most places, but has a tasteless sexual connotation in Australia.

While there are literally hundreds of these things to be cautious about, being an American, French, German, Brazilian, or any nationality often gives you some degree of exemption. People will say, "What do they know, they're from America (or France, or Germany, or Brazil)."

## Other Protocols

You will undoubtedly find Europeans to be a bit more formal than Americans, and you may want to be a little bit reserved on introductions, i.e., never address European business associates by their first names unless they suggest it to you. Further, try to be firm but not too firm a handshake.

British companies are still hierarchical in management, and you should respect that custom when it is evident. But you can use first names with care in Britain. Do not discuss the royal family in any way other than politely and with respect. Only Australians can call Britain's queen "Betty Windsor."

French businesspeople are formal and, like the British, will not appreciate your "dropping in" without a proper appointment. The business day seems to start late, about 9:30 A.M. There is a break for a long lunch, and then business resumes until past 6. Don't discuss personal issues with French associates.

Italy is like most Latin countries where your success will depend on developing a relationship. Never refuse an invitation to an Italian meal because it shows a lack of good taste on your part, and you will miss some great food!

Germans, as expected, are punctual, and will appreciate punctuality from you. Don't try to organize a breakfast meeting in Germany; they are too obsessive about working.

A great deal in this book covers Japan, primarily because that culture is so complicated for Westerners. Business cards are a must upon meeting for the first time, and it is more than likely that your airline can imprint the blank side of your existing cards in Japanese if you give your airline people enough time. Japanese executives tend to dress in blue suits, white shirts, and conservative ties, so don't be flamboyant. Bring others with you when you negotiate, and be sure someone you know can be there to help translate.

In China a great deal of advance planning is necessary to set up meeting dates, but the Chinese will be cordial and quite willing to work and bargain with you to the fairest outcome for both sides. Be prepared in China and Japan to drink a great deal of hot tea!

## Specific Sensitivities

In a German business office, the boss will have his door closed and be addressed as Mister. This is very normal protocol; you should respect it in the office regardless of your relationship to the management when others are present. But after hours you can revert to the informality with which you may be familiar.

In the People's Republic of China, do not expect anyone in any meeting to admire any material possession you might have with you to the point where you may feel that you want to offer it as a gift. Do not leave a pen as a gift because that action seems to imply to some people that they don't have one!

Lots of luck at a Chinese banquet, where you may be offered sea slug soup, bear paw as a delicacy, a goose foot in your soup, and heaven knows what else! These "delicacies" were quite expensive for your host, and any negative feelings you might have should be saved for the plane ride home. In Scandinavia, be sure to look your host in the eye when you and he are toasting one another, but don't have a lot of eye contact in Japan because it may be construed as an insult or an invasion of privacy.

## GIFT GIVING

Pens seem to be a very popular gift almost anywhere in the world except China. A nice pen as a gift can avoid several issues that might otherwise be a problem. First, whether the symbols are Arabic, Japanese, Cyrillic or like ours (in the Latin alphabet), everyone writes and can use a pen. Second, pens are easy to carry when you travel from place to place. While Cross pens are a hit, think about the culture you are visiting. Many Japanese look at metal pens as too cold and almost indifferent in appearance. A pen clad in wood might be ideal in Japan, but also remember that the Japanese prefer fine writing tips and black ink because they communicate in symbols or ideographs.

The subject of gift giving in a country like Japan has been worked over by every expert in the field. If you are at all perplexed about gift giving for Japanese customers or friends, the following comments may be of interest:

In general, gift giving in Japan is intended to create some sort of aura for the giver, the gift, and the recipient. That aura can be interpreted generally as "a sense of goodwill or an expression of some level of relationship." One level of gift giving is simply passing on a token which, in effect, tells the recipient you think enough of them to offer them a remembrance of the meeting. Often, that remembrance will, in turn, be passed on to someone else by the person to whom you gave the gift.

A level beyond the simple gift is a company or organization gift, i.e., something given not by an individual, even though it may be handed to you by one person, but rather a gift representing an expression of regard from a company or organization. Sometimes this gift may be left at your hotel; at other times it may be something you admired that your hosts then purchased for you. The latter is very important and significant because there sometimes is a tendency, from either giver or receiver, to look at a gift given this way as a bribe (and it may well be).

Finally, when there is a sincere bond of friendship with someone, a gift of meaning (not necessarily something of great value) tells your friend that you value the friendship. There are also guidelines of good taste and manners whenever gifts are given:

1. Let your Japanese counterpart make the first move in gift giving. Even if you have brought something, wait to see what he does. You may embarrass him by offering a gift when he has nothing for you.
2. July 15 and January 1 are mandatory gift days in Japan.
3. Think about having different grades of gifts so you don't "outgive" a Japanese. That is very rude and doesn't show much style on your part.
4. Don't open your gift in front of the giver. Have something for everyone at a meeting or wait until you and your host are alone. Remember, form is everything.
5. Don't be too enthusiastic about the gift you receive; be reserved in your thanks.
6. Don't feel you have been treated poorly if the gift you receive is either inexpensive or not practical; the giving is the key!
7. Wrapping a gift is important. Never give an unwrapped or poorly wrapped gift. Avoid using brightly colored paper; don't use ribbons and bows; avoid black, white, or red paper and ribbons and offer a gift with both hands.
8. Avoid multiples of fours, e.g., four cocktail glasses; the number has bad meanings.
9. Don't use promotional gimmicks as gifts, e.g., tee shirts with a company name, imprinted cheap pens, and caps. Rather think about giving branded U.S. merchandise, which has a quality connotation.

In Latin American countries never go to someone's home without a gift; a large plant or flower bouquet can be perfect. Gift giving is not done during business, and there is a great sensitivity to the possibility of doing something that might be construed as a bribe. Get to know your Latin American associates before you think about giving a gift at other times than when you go to their homes.

In Middle Eastern countries gift giving, to be safe, should

probably focus on items for your colleague's children. Never offer whiskey since it is against the Islamic religion, and be careful not to admire something your host has or he might give it to you. Arabs are wonderful hosts who really seem to cherish relationships when they are genuine.

## ON TRYING NEW THINGS

After visiting Finland a few times and wondering about saunas, I approached my host one day and asked if he could arrange a sauna for me at my hotel that evening. He immediately left the room and returned a few minutes later with the news that I had an appointment at 8:30 that evening for a sauna in the hotel. He had a rather peculiar smile on his face, however, when I asked him what I should wear to the sauna. He looked at me in my blue suit and challis print tie, and suggested I go as I was; the people in the sauna would tell me what to do.

At the appropriate time, I walked up to the reception desk in the sauna and told the rather attractive young lady who I was. In my nervousness I blurted out that it was my first sauna, and the same impish smile appeared on her face that I had seen earlier with my host. She directed me down the hall to a room marked simply "3." The room consisted of a hallway leading into a dressing (or undressing) room that faced a beautiful lake. Off to one side of the hall was a wooden door, and behind that door presumably was "my" sauna for that time period.

After about five minutes a very old lady came in, seemingly surprised to see me standing there. Since she spoke no English, and I no Finnish, she motioned that I should remove my clothing and enter the sauna. She left, I grabbed a fingertip towel and did as I was apparently instructed.

The room was unbearably hot; the towel was all that prevented my body from fusing itself to the platform upon which I was sitting; and after about 10 minutes, I decided I'd had enough. No sooner had I walked out of the sauna than the attendant returned. She motioned with 10 fingers that I apparently had 10 more minutes in the sauna, and back I went.

After that additional 10 minutes I was told to lie down on a marble slab in the room while the dear old lady scrubbed me with some ridiculously abrasive material. After a shower I was handed a very skimpy bathing suit, and she pointed out the door.

Outside was a green, shimmering pool of water waiting for my heated, pulsating body. I could hear other hotel guests, presumably Finnish, coming down the hall toward the pool, and for "the honor of my country" I felt I had to put on a brave show. I jumped into the pool.

Going down toward the bottom of the pool and then drifting slowly back to the top was one of the longest periods of my life. I will always remember the temperature of that water (cold) and the bubbles drifting past my head as I wondered what madness had caused me to go to a sauna in Finland. Yet I was destined to go twice more—on a boat to Sweden where I sagely warned a fellow American *not* to sit at the top of the seating lest he cook too soon, and in the Finnish countryside where my hosts and I "enjoyed" a Finnish country sauna, complete with sausages hanging and cooking from the ceiling along with us and a dip into a frozen lake across the border from Russia.

### Why Is Everyone So Clean?

A sauna in Finland, a bath in Japan. What's the difference—except everything is more to the Western scale in Scandinavia. At a Japanese bath I went to in Hakone, the "bath" was water from a little bucket, the "soak" was in a series of pools afterward, and, as in Finland, my host and I completed the occasion with beer and sushi (versus sausage in Finland). The sense of friendship that develops from doing these things that your host does as part of his (or her?) life adds significantly to the relationships essential for long-term business development in any culture of the world.

What can a woman do, however, in these situations?

### Alternatives for Women and Less Venturesome Men

The simplest way to enjoy another culture when you travel on business is to be somewhat daring with food and/or with language.

A great many Oriental and Middle Eastern dishes are now generally found in the United States, and you should consider a few restaurant excursions before a trip abroad in order to familiarize yourself with some of the basic foods. Sushi is still sushi whether it's in Kyoto or Portland, and some Chinese dishes exist in virtually every Far Eastern country because the Chinese have migrated throughout that area. A note of caution, however: Chinese food in the People's Republic of China is not like the Chinese food with which you are familiar!

This same technique can be used with Latin American and European foods, and the results are that you can comfortably ask for specific things in restaurants and at dinners abroad after you have, in effect, sampled them here. Please be a bit more daring though!

### Try a Little Language

A trick to success in some places is to learn a bit of the language. Failing that, another device is on-the-job learning. While phonetic spelling is not my forte, here are a few ways of asking, "How do you say (whatever) in (language)?"

- *German.* "Wie sagt man das auf Deutsch?"
  "How do you say that in German?"
- *Japanese.* "Nee Hongo de (whatever) nanto i mas ka?"
  "How do you say (whatever) in Japanese?"
- *Chinese.* "Chung kwo wha, tsen mo sure (whatever)?"
  *Mandarin.* "How do you say (whatever) in Chinese?"
- *Spanish.* "Como se dice (whatever) en español?"
  "How do you say (whatever) in Spanish?"
- *French.* "Comment dit-on (whatever) en français?"
  "How do you say (whatever) in French?"
- *Russian.* "Kak skazat po Rooskie (whatever)."
  "How do you say (whatever) in Russian?"

This little phrase will help you build a vocabulary in another language, and will assuredly help develop rapport with the people with whom you are involved.

## Some Additional Thoughts on Food for You Too

Because of the tremendous growth in ethnic restaurants in this country, which has been fostered by the recent influxes of Asians and Latins, it is relatively easy to become familiar with the subtleties of different cultures and the in foods. Be prepared, however, for some delicacies you may not relish.

At a large dinner in Sweden, the first course began with a bright red meat on an appetizer plate, apparently in the form of a piece of sausage. When I asked my host what the meat was, he told me it was horse meat, a delicacy (I guess) in Sweden. Fortunately, I remembered his inability to eat the peanut butter I had brought him as a gift. When I told him I didn't think I could eat the horse meat, my first rationale dealt with his lack of desire for peanut butter. That didn't seem to satisfy him, and I resorted to a comment I have yet to live down. I told him eating horse meat in America was a cultural problem because "cowboys didn't eat their transportation."

## Some Minor Tricks of the Trade in Eating/ Drinking Abroad

Some Asian foods are extremely spicy. Even your hosts don't have supertough taste buds, and you should notice that generally there is also fresh-cut fruit somewhere on the table. A small piece of melon or other similar fruit will extinguish the fire of spices far better than gallons of water or ice cubes resting on your tongue in the privacy of your closed mouth.

Middle Eastern foods remind me of going to a health food store. All the grains, mashed or otherwise, along with subtle tastes of mint, and the pita you will be served as well as the lamb, are delicious, delightful—and never a worry. Islam has very strict dietary laws that will preclude some of the truly exotic items you may find elsewhere. This is also true in Israel where the Jewish kosher laws are virtually identical.

European tastes are pretty much the same as ours except for the once-in-a-while bit of horse meat. You will always find some things on the menu that meet your taste.

In Latin America you will also find a great many items similar to those you know. Depending on the country, you will surely enjoy great beef (Argentina), seafood (Peru), shellfish (Chile), or whatever the local specialties might be.

## WHAT ABOUT TIPPING?

Tipping is a way of life in the United States, and we all know that some waiters and waitresses live literally on the tips they earn in restaurants. Other countries can be quite different, however, and I remember the amazement on our Australian sales agent's wife's face after she'd had her hair done in the United States and simply walked out of the salon. She had no idea that the shampoo person and the hairdresser were expecting a tip because there was none of that in Australia. The converse of this, of course, is the Australian cab driver I once tipped. He gave me the money back, announcing that he earned enough with the fare!

So, in *Australia,* tipping is not customary, not even with hotel porters. There may be preestablished per bag charges for air or rail porters, but you will see them. In a restaurant, however, a 10 percent tip is expected, but that's it down under!

In the *People's Republic of China,* tips are absolutely offensive to people.

In *Hong Kong,* at least until 1997 but probably thereafter as well, restaurants will probably add a 10 percent service charge to your bill, and you might wish to leave a little extra. I tip porters, and taxi drivers will assuredly expect a 5 to 10 percent tip.

*Japan* does not like tipping, and hotel porters used to look at me strangely when I first went there and proffered a tip. Your hotel bill might well reflect a service charge, however, so it all seems to level out in the end. Restaurants will do the same.

In *Europe* generally, a service charge will probably be on your restaurant bill, and you will see it. Leaving a small, extra amount of change will indicate to the server that the treatment you received merited more. Taxi drivers will expect a tip generally, and so too will porters—10 to 15 percent for a taxi and about 50 cents per bag are satisfactory.

In the *Soviet Union,* a tip will most likely be added to your bill, or it may not even be expected. Tipping is not expected by hotel porters, taxi drivers, or even tour guides. But a real treat might be a small, typically American gift for someone you expect will be doing you a special favor or service. In this category think about a small bottle of American perfume, a small amount of an unusual sweet, or even a nice ball pen (not with your company logo on it!).

In *Latin America* generally, you should travel with a lot of U.S. $1 bills. These are clearly the tip of choice as inflation continues to devastate the local currency. Whenever you are in doubt in Latin America, leave a tip, and be gracious.

## SOME EXTRANEOUS OTHER RECOLLECTIONS

Don't ever find yourself having to buy an airplane ticket in Japan; the price will be almost double what it is almost anywhere else. Try not to shop in Tokyo where the prices will astound you.

Stay out of so-called barber shops in Taipei unless you want a lot more than a haircut!

If you are the only passenger in a taxi in Australia, sit in the front seat with the driver. This very egalitarian country, where you won't tip the driver, expects you to treat him like the right kind of bloke he is!

Don't take a rickshaw ride in Hong Kong unless you want to have to have your picture taken and then be gouged for a round-the-block ride.

Remember not to wear socks with holes when you are in Japan because you probably will be taking your shoes off before you enter a restaurant, shrine, or various other institutions (including people's homes if you are really lucky).

While socks with holes were never a cause of embarrassment for me in Japan, an idiosyncrasy with my shoes was. A long time ago I had read you should not wear the same shoes every day. It apparently prolonged their life if you let them air out for a day between wearings. Dutifully, I dragged two pairs of shoes on overseas trips.

Once, on a short trip to Japan, however, I simply didn't feel like carrying a great amount of luggage. I took my required blue suit for business in Tokyo and only one pair of shoes, along with a can of foot powder that I planned to use to keep my feet feeling comfortable.

On the second day of the trip, I put on my only pair of shoes for the second day in a row, but first I tossed in great amounts of white foot powder.

After meeting with a customer of our distributor, the suggestion was made that we all go to lunch, and off we went to a restaurant where it was obligatory that I remove my shoes at the door. Naturally, I had long forgotten the foot powder.

As we were being shown to our table at the rear of the restaurant, normally polite and quiet Japanese customers began giggling as I walked by. Only when I looked back and saw that I was leaving a trail of perfectly formed white footprints all the way from the front door to the back of the restaurant did I understand why I never should have used foot powder in Japan!

## SUMMARY

Being interested in the food and the language of your hosts, as well as trying to be aware of the differences between your culture to theirs—all this will give you an opportunity to make lifelong friendships in addition to helping build your business. The business you can establish with these efforts at showing your host (your customer, if you wish) that you are interested and care will always enhance your potential in a market compared to gruff, disinterested persons who quickly show by deed and emotion that they do not want to be wherever they are.

I never saw other Americans at the baths in Japan, but others surely must do it. There were never Americans in Finnish saunas, but they always talked about trying the coeducational ones in Germany. Too many Americans bring their own coffee jars and even canned foods to China to win many friends there. Even the few Americans left who smoke don't seem to try the local brands in any country, preferring Marlboro. While Phillip Morris may like that, what are you telling your hosts about their country and its products?

# CHAPTER 14

# YOU'VE SOLD IT, NOW SHIP IT!

## or "WHAT DO ALL THESE TERMS MEAN?"

One of the seemingly greatest impediments to any firm's desire to move into the export arena is the issue of payment and shipping. Too many times there have been managers voicing the opinion that it is just too difficult to deal with the paperwork for shipping and/or that they have no idea how anyone gets paid.

### TIME TO RELAX ON GETTING PAID

There are a few ways you can develop payment plans with your customers, and be sure that those plans are detailed in your contract so there is no confusion.

First, if an account is credit-trustworthy, e.g., part of a major corporation where you can obtain credit verification and assurances by way of a bank or reputable credit agency, you can always sell on open account if you wish. Open account, with terms you and the customer agree to (remember there is shipping time of a greater length than domestically) based on order cycles, delivery times, etc., can be one way of showing a customer that you and he will operate in an area of open trust. Payment terms of 30 days, 60 days, and 90 days are all quite common in the export business, but be sure there is an ability to pay.

## WHAT'S A LETTER OF CREDIT?

Letters of credit are used on occasion in this country between seller and buyer when there is a strong concern about the credit-worthiness of the buyer. In effect, the buyer posts an amount equivalent to the value of the purchase with his or her bank. As soon as the goods arrive, but before they are delivered to the buyer's premises, they are checked to insure completeness. The buyer's bank then notifies the seller and his bank that the funds will be transferred.

Letters of credit can be limited in duration, e.g., a 60-day letter, which means you will have 60 days to deliver the goods, etc., but this device is the surest way to insure you will be paid until you truly know your customer and his credit worthiness.

## WHAT'S FOB OR CIF?

FOB simply means "free on board." There are several FOB ways to ship:

1. *FOB port of exit.* The seller's price includes all expenses from the factory onto the ship.
2. *FOB cars or FOB alongside.* The seller's price includes all expenses from the factory to the port, but loading is at the buyer's expense.
3. *FOB port of entry, duty paid.* As the name implies, the seller's price includes everything from the factory all the way to the port of entry of the buyer, including payment of duty.
4. *FOB factory.* The buyer starts paying right after the goods leave the line or the warehouse, i.e., inland freight, etc. to the port.

CIF represents initials for "cost"(C), "insurance"(I), and "freight"(F). An order may arrive CIF port, which means that you will pay costs, insurance, and freight to the port of entry, after which the buyer is liable. Sometimes the terms are C&F, excluding insurance, and the buyer provides his own insurance.

CIF duty paid or FOB duty paid means exactly what the terms define.

## Then Costs Will Be Different, Domestic versus Export

Probably true, but this will depend on how you wish to do things. Depending upon who has agreed to pay for what, the real differences in pricing will be in export documentation fees, ocean freight and insurance, import duties and taxes, and the time and money you may wish to invest in your own personnel or those of an export management company necessary to handle documentation from start to finish.

Documentation will probably start with the buyer's request for a pro-forma invoice. This is a document that will tell the buyer what to expect in terms of cost when the goods you have sold are received. The following items belong in the pro-forma invoice:

1. Obviously the buyer's name, address, and country.
2. An inquiry date and an expiration date after which the quotation is invalid.
3. A listing of the products to be ordered with prices for each and in total, in U.S. dollars.
4. Gross and net weight and the total cube of the shipment.
5. Any discount and terms, including payment terms.
6. Insurance and all shipping costs, inland and sea, if applicable.
7. Point of delivery.
8. Total charges of the order that are to the buyer's account.
9. Estimated shipping and arrival dates.

Not everyone will need this much documentation. Once you begin a continuing relationship and your overseas customer knows what he or she is dealing with in terms of prices, costs, volumes, weights, etc., the customer may simply send you an order, requesting that it be delivered to his freight forwarder or agent in this country. The forwarder or agent will then deal with the paperwork, and you can begin the invoicing process.

## How Can You Finance the Deal with Safety?

As you may learn, you will want your money as soon as possible while your customer may want to hold back as long as possible. Now that the above terms have been laid out, an anecdote is in order.

Before we established a distributor in Australia, I had received a letter with a U.S. dollar bill enclosed and a request for a product catalog. In preparing for a serious sales strategy in Australia, we had begun to develop a special product for that market, but we weren't quite ready to find a full-fledged distributor.

The letter and dollar intrigued me, and we sent off a catalog, suggesting that the buyer keep the dollar in readiness to partially pay for his first order. Shortly thereafter, I received a written order worth about $125 accompanied by a bank draft and a request that the goods be air-freighted to Australia. I was more than slightly embarrassed at the small size of the order, but dutifully dispatched it.

Within a month another order arrived, again with a bank draft, but this time it was five times as large, and it was still to go by air freight. Off it went, and I then started receiving very lengthy phone calls from the people who were conducting business in this very peculiar manner. Phone calls overseas are never inexpensive, and Australia is not a stone's throw away!

A third order arrived, this time nearly half a small container load; the bank draft was with the order, and my instructions for shipping had now been changed—the mystery customer was going to use a ship this time! I was within a month of traveling to Australia to line up a distributor, and when this unusual customer phoned me, I suggested we meet in Sydney. There was a bit of a gasp at the other end of the line, and I was sure the meeting would prove to be quite a treat.

The mystery buyer, it developed, was four young men who loved cars. One worked for a bank, which explained the drafts; another for the phone company, and that covered the lengthy calls; and a third ran his own small repair shop. These three, plus a fourth friend, had pooled their resources to pay for the first order, bought it at a very competitive price, and sold the goods to the final user at full retail, bypassing the entire distribution system and all of its commissions.

They then turned the profits into their second, larger order and did exactly the same thing. The last order, by sea, was to represent their biggest gamble: they were using the ship as a floating warehouse, hoping they could sell the entire inventory before the ship docked!

## You've Got to Maintain a Sense of Customer Worth

After we arranged for a legitimate national distributor in Australia, I felt I owed these four entrepreneurs some special consideration. By mutual agreement with the new national distributor, the four young men were to get the best available pricing from our distributor as long as they remained in business, buying now from our local warehouse.

Why? Because people respect initiative, ambition, and hard work. These young men had demonstrated to me and our distributor that a great new market awaited us, and it didn't seem fair—in this case in the British or Australian sense—to turn our backs on them after they had risked almost every penny they had to see if the market would accept our U.S. product.

## More on Documentation (Don't Panic!)

There are a great many reasons to document thoroughly all information concerning a shipment. The fact of the matter is that you are sending something of value to a strange land on a vessel you will probably never see, to be inspected and/or accepted by government officials you don't know. Naturally, you want to be paid fairly for that which was ordered and sent.

The first obvious issues you must deal with are adequate packing to withstand the rigors of a long trip and appropriate insurance taken out by you or the buyer. Documentation will be the key to verification that all conditions, contents, and concerns are met.

## How to Start

A good starting point is a solid international freight forwarder that will act on your behalf and assist you with the necessary documentation and follow-through on your shipment. The freight forwarder can provide you with freight costs, insurance costs, local importer rules and regulations, and a myriad of other situations that might otherwise scare off a serious exporter.

The U.S. Department of Commerce lists the following documents an exporter might face; each can be dealt with by an international forwarder:

- Commercial invoice. You are probably already familiar with this common document, which in this case is used in assessing import duties.
- Bill of lading. This document is similar to a domestic bill of lading. Two types of export bills of lading exist: straight bills and negotiable bills. The latter can be bought, sold, or traded; they are generally involved in letter-of-credit transactions.
- Certificate of origin. Simply a signed document verifying the origin of the goods.
- Inspection certificate. This document does just what the name implies. Australia, for example, won't admit pallets of used wood in a shipment. The inspection certificate verifies the fact that the wood is new and unused.
- Destination control statement. It certifies that the goods in transit will go only to a specified destination.
- Insurance certificate. It states the type and amount of insurance coverage.
- Shipper's export declaration. This document, which is used for shipments valued at more than $500, is basically used in compiling export statistics.
- Export license. This important document insures that certain items of a critical nature, such as defense materials, have been approved for export.
- Packing list. It describes each package in detail: the container; its contents; the net, legal, tare, and gross weight; and other measurements.

## More Detail on Getting Paid

Not everyone will send along a bank draft the way my young Australian friends did. The fundamental methods of payment in the export business are as follow:

Cash in advance. The method is best for you, but maybe not for the buyer.

Letter of credit(L/C). Discussed earlier, this is a solid way to do it.

Drafts. There are two kinds of drafts: (1) those calling for sight payment via documents; and (2) time-payment drafts calling for payment within a specified time.

Open account. As previously discussed, this method is used for solid credit risks or as a reward or goal for a good payment history on the part of the buyer.

Consignment. Don't use this method. If there's no investment, then there's no incentive to sell!

## What's a Duty Drawback?

Traditionally a drawback is a refunded duty or tax, in whole or in part, because of a particular use made of an item or commodity that has been taxed initially.

There are several types of drawbacks, and if your business becomes a two-way street, with imports and exports, you should surely know about drawbacks:

1. When an article exported from the United States has been manufactured in this country with the use of some imported items, the duties originally paid on the imported items may be refunded as a drawback, less 1 percent to defray U.S. customs costs.
2. If both imported and domestic merchandise of an identical kind and quality have been used to produce your products, and some of the products are exported, a drawback not in excess of 99 percent of the duty paid on the imported merchandise is payable on the exported goods. It doesn't matter whether the imported or domestic mer-

chandise was actually used in the exported merchandise. This is a boon to inventory management in that you don't have to maintain separate inventories of imported and domestic raw materials or keep special records, etc., in order to obtain a drawback.

3. If merchandise is exported because it does not conform with sample specifications or was shipped without the consent of the consignee, 99 percent of the duties originally paid may be recovered as a drawback.
4. When certain items are produced in this country with domestic alcohol and then exported to various island possessions, a drawback is available on the internal revenue tax paid on domestic alcohol.
5. If imported salt is used to cure fish, the duties on the salt are covered. Further, if imported salt is used to cure meat which is then exported, a drawback can be obtained in amounts not less than $100 of the duties paid on the salt.
6. If imported materials are used to construct and equip vessels and aircraft built for foreign ownership, 99 percent of the duties on the imported materials may be covered by drawback.
7. If imported merchandise is used in this country to repair foreign-made jet aircraft engines, the duties on the merchandise may be subject to drawback in amounts not less than $100 as soon as the engines are exported.
8. If imported merchandise is exported in the same condition or if it is destroyed under U.S. customs supervision in the same condition as it was imported, there is a 99 percent drawback on the duties paid.

## How to Obtain a Drawback

You will have to prepare a drawback proposal and file it with the regional Commissioner of Customs or with the drawback and bonds branch, Customs Headquarters, depending upon the type of drawback for which you qualify. A phone call to U.S. Customs at (202) 566–5856 will get you going in the right direction.

# APPENDIX

## DISC IS GONE, FSC IS IN: A QUICK OUTLINE ON SETTING UP A FOREIGN SALES CORPORATION (FSC)

Before the Tax Reform Act of 1984, U.S. companies could operate DISCs, that is, domestic corporations that could shield export-generated income in large measure from taxation. Our trading partners felt that was an unfair advantage (I will strongly fight the urge to comment here on their feelings), and Congress curtailed DISC benefits while creating something called a Foreign Sales Corporation (FSC).

Unlike a DISC, which was a domestic corporation, a FSC has to be a foreign corporation. A DISC was not taxable; a FSC is a taxpaying entity that enjoys a certain exemption of certain income from U.S. taxation.

The method of exemption for a FSC is simply to treat foreign-trade income as foreign-source income not effectively connected with the conduct of a trade or business within the United States.

To qualify as a FSC operation, the following criteria have to be met:

1. The firm must be a corporation created or organized under the laws of any U.S. possession or under the laws of any foreign country that has an appropriate agreement or income tax treaty. (Puerto Rico, by the way, is not considered a U.S. possession, but the U.S. Virgin Islands are.)
2. There must be 25 or less shareholders.
3. There can be no outstanding preferred stock.
4. The FSC must maintain an office in any U.S. possession or appropriate foreign country, and this office need not be in the country of incorporation.
5. The FSC must maintain a set of permanent accounts (including invoices) at the office described above.
6. The FSC must maintain records at a United States location also.
7. The firm's board of directors must have at least one member who is not a U.S. resident. This person can, however, be a U.S. citizen.

8. The FSC cannot be a part of a corporation any part of which has been represented as a DISC.
9. The business unit must have an election, in effect, to be treated as a FSC. Further, the taxable year of the FSC must be the same as that of its principal shareholders (the parent company).

In summary, these criteria look harder than they really are. As soon as you develop any export presence, a FSC can be established quite easily in a convenient market or nearby U.S. possession so as to help with tax issues.

For more information, refer to the *Guide to International Commerce Law*, edited by Paul H. Vishny (New York: McGraw-Hill, 1981).

# CHAPTER 15

# SOME THOUGHTS FOR THE EEC—NOW + 1992

## or "EVERY EXTRA CAPABILITY COUNTS"

Earlier in this book I talked a bit about a market research project conducted in Germany to determine our brand's awareness and acceptance within its own distribution system while, competing with German-made products, Belgian products, some Japanese products, and British-made products.

While that discussion focused generally on price versus other issues that tended to impact on a product's success, the reader may recall that I was almost caught up short by our German sales manager's comments from the field that, because the newly introduced British product was the lowest in price, we "had" to lower our prices.

Fortunately, the research helped us avoid a bad mistake, i.e., imitating the lower British price because no one in Germany was even willing to buy the British product. That's a point worth thinking about as we consider the end of 1992 and the European Economic Community.

As you may already know, the deadline set by the European Parliament for creating a single market for the 12 nations of the EEC is 1992. This means that some 300 directives will be implemented in order to eliminate trade barriers and to create consistent product standards among the EEC nations. (See Chapter 10 for a bit more information about standards.)

## ONE QUICK OBSERVATION

The *Washington Post National Weekly Edition* for March 27 to April 2, 1989 characterized some issues in the EEC markets as follow:

- Great Britain. The British fear that scrapping border controls will make it easier for terrorists and other criminals to enter the country.
- Ireland. This country should receive significant help in its economic adjustment.
- Denmark. The Danes have mixed emotions about leaving other Scandinavians in the lurch while they join their continental partners in the EEC.
- The Netherlands. A strong infrastructure with healthy trucking and shipping facilities should benefit the Dutch.
- Belgium. This is the headquarters of the EEC and home of the "Eurocrats."
- Luxembourg. This country hopes to become a major EEC banking center.
- West Germany. The Germans look to expand their production and sales into southern Europe. But the highly regulated German insurance industry worries about new competitive pressures.
- France. The classic chauvanism of the French has expanded to include all of Europe.
- Portugal. This country looks for a dynamic change and an infusion of energy and ideas.
- Spain. Lower wages in Spain might mean that other countries will expand their production facilities into this area.
- Italy. The Italians have mixed feelings about competition and their ability to operate efficiently, given their big bureaucracy.
- Greece. Because of their less developed economy, the Greeks have some concern about truly fitting in and enjoying the benefits.

## A Marketplace of Millions, Sales for Some

When you reflect on the European community over any period of time, you can immediately see that each country has very chauvinistically endeavored, for the most part, to develop its own identity in certain industries.

Cars, for example, are produced in Italy, France, Germany, and Great Britain. But should Fiat (Italy) or Renault (France) or Ford (U.K.) or Ford (Germany) or GM Opel (Germany) think that the world has opened up to them simply because the trade barriers are gone? Would any self-respecting German buy a Fiat or a Renault (a few do!)? How many more British buyers will there be for Renault or Peugeot? And what happens to SEAT, the Spanish Fiat?

Whose TV sets will be preeminent in this new market? Or washers and dryers? Or vacuum cleaners? Most of the major countries produce for local consumption, but the lure of selling EEC-wise will have to be great.

German beer with its long-time purity law was found to be creating an illegal obstacle for trade for other European brewers who don't follow the same strict ingredient policies. Watching changes in the brewing industry will surely be fascinating.

In Spain, Campsa, the marketing arm of the state-owned oil company, recently concluded a deal with 7-Eleven Convenience Food Stores to set up minimarts at their Spanish service stations. Why? To offset the arrival of other-country fuel brands.

European companies are already maneuvering to take advantage of joint ventures, acquisitions, mergers, and consolidations—whatever will insure a broader success after 1992. The result surely will be fewer companies with greater financial assets and a much more competitive environment.

If this isn't enough, imagine the ideological differences that already exist between the free-market countries of Great Britain and West Germany versus the Socialist Mediterranean countries led by France's Mitterand. There are reports that airline deregulation and protected industries are the battlelines where these two groups will ultimately face off against each other.

## Perceptions Can Be Everything

Just as buyers at every level tend to discriminate now, so too will they in the future. That's where the true opportunities for economic gain will develop in the EEC. In real estate opportunities alone, the United States has already dipped its toe in, and probably justifiably: some of the finest architectural and developmental deals are created here.

In Birmingham, England, a $136 million, 450,000 square foot festival market and entertainment center has been developed by the same people who designed Baltimore's Harbor Place. Europe's tallest office building—70 stories with nearly three-quarters of a million square feet of office space—has been designed for Frankfurt, West Germany, by Helmut Jahn, a Chicago architect, and is being developed by Tishman Speyer Properties, a New York-based company.

A New York development firm, American Continental Properties, is putting together a European real estate investment fund from U.S. pension funds. The firm is also developing a 500,000 square foot project in Rome—a landmark brewery less than a mile from the Via Veneto that will be a mixed-use combination of offices, stores, and condominiums.

Ford, GM, and IBM are preeminently ready for 1992 because of their present-day strength in Europe generally. Ford and GM are the only automobile manufacturers (with the possible exception of Fiat and its arrangements in Spain) currently operating across borders as European automotive companies, and IBM, with $20 billion in sales in Europe, leads its nearest competitor, Siemens of West Germany, by a factor of four; IBM has quadruple the sales of Siemens.

## But You Have to Know the Ropes

In the case of real estate development, most developers will tell you that it is harder to deal in Europe than in America because of land-use patterns based on population densities and local codes. In Great Britain pension funds are invested more heavily in real estate than they are currently in the United States. That tends to alter control elements a bit. The attraction for real estate has to be both its challenge and financial reward: office rents in London range as much as four times higher than those in Chicago, while Amsterdam's rents might be half as much as Chicago's.

Because of consistent product standards in the EEC, opportunities for pharmaceutical companies will be greatly improved. Instead of seeking 12 different approvals for new product introductions, only one will be needed in the future. Some firms believe that this will reduce their product rollouts by up to three years.

### The Value of the Right Partner

In the case of the EEC and the future, success surely will be based on the people with whom you have aligned yourself, not simply your presence in the marketplace.

It will be very important for the image and customer perception across borders to be consistent and not totally a unilateral, one-country situation. Otherwise, your risks may never reap a reward.

Remember that the EEC consists of Belgium, France, Italy, Luxembourg, the Netherlands, West Germany, the United Kingdom, Denmark, Ireland, Greece, Spain, and Portugal. (It does not include Sweden, Finland, Norway, or Switzerland.) Look at opportunities and investments in terms of broad-based acceptance into any or all these countries, not just one or two.

### It Won't Be a Bed of Roses for a While

While everyone talks about a pan-European market of great buying and selling power, there remain handicaps to be overcome:

- There is no common language among the 12 countries.
- There will be, but there isn't yet, a common currency.
- A disparity of legal concepts is yet to be resolved.
- The EEC today is not a single market; there are still 12 sets of rules, with companies in each country producing only for their home market. (Imagine a company produc-

ing only for Ohio!) And there are barriers to real business growth, including (1) varying technical specifications that need to be standarized; (2) varying health and safety standards in plants; and (3) differences in indirect taxation.

The issue then becomes one of determining how, when, where, and why the real impact will occur—an impact in cost savings; greater employment because of expanded demand, increased competition from within and the outside; lower prices as a result; dynamic market growth in competition with other major markets of the world.

### American Companies Preparing to Do It Well

There are several well-managed U.S. companies with a European presence through export and/or joint venturing that are positioning themselves now for 1992 and beyond. The following are suggested only to offer some ideas for the kind of thinking probably necessary to do very well in the EEC.

- MasterCard has purchased a 15 percent share of its European counterpart, Eurocard, thus providing MasterCard with a bit more influence in its overall strategic marketing plans in Europe.
- Johnson & Johnson recently rolled out Silhouettes feminine hygiene products, approaching Europe as one market rather than markets in several different countries.
- Johnson Wax has realigned most of its brands in Europe in household and personal care products to begin implementing an all-Europe brand strategy for each product line.
- U.S. firms are breaking down multiple advertising agency relationships in favor of a select few more suitable to dealing with Europe as a totality rather than as different markets.

The marketing efforts of major U.S. brands will probably also complement smaller, regional products in Europe. General Mills's Yoplait and Dannon yogurt have paved the way for Greek-produced yogurt products on the continent. Nestlé, by the way, with three different yogurt brand names in Europe, recently added the name *Nestlé* to each, presumably as a transition to one Nestlé brand after 1992!

## Current Information Sources

The EEC office in New York City claims to be publishing a newsletter; several major accounting firms claim to be offering seminars. As the end of 1992 draws closer, more and more apparent resources will spring to life. But if you want to think about the planning process now, one resource is available from a U.S. advertising agency, Bozell, Jacobs, Kenyon & Eckhardt. It is a computer-available program called SCOPE 1992 (**S**ystems **C**oordinated for **P**lanning and **E**fficiency).

SCOPE 1992 is designed to help you plan for real expansion into the EEC and to help you understand and deal with competition.

The following pages represent the worksheets for France for SCOPE 1992. A diskette with sufficient market information for each of the 12 EEC member countries is available with sufficient statistical data on each country, its current laws, its media, its media costs, its prohibitions in terms of advertising and/or promotion. Planning now may help when the final rules are in place for the EEC in 1992.

# B-O-Z-E-L-L INTERNATIONAL SCOPE 1992*

## Systems Coordinated for Planning Efficiency

### *SCOPE 1992: France*

Scope *n* 1. space or opportunity for unhampered motion, activity, or thought. 2. extent of treatment, activity, or influence. 3. range of operation.

SCOPE 1992 has been developed by BOZELL, an international advertising agency, to help companies plan for expansion made more attractive by the EEC's 1992 legislation. SCOPE 1992 can also help companies defend themselves from international competition resulting from that same legislation.

This outline is not meant to be a rigid guide, but rather a kind of workbook that can be adapted to the needs of almost any company. We recognize that corporations can be vastly different from one another, both in their objectives and methods of operation. Further, the approaches to different product categories will also vary. But SCOPE 1992 can be a useful tool in planning to meet the challenges of marketing in the EEC in the years to come.

### *SCOPE 1992 MENU*

A. Target country data
B. Market profile
C. Problems and opportunities
D. Objectives
E. Strategy development
F. Restrictions
G. Communications plan outline

---

*SCOPE 1992 was prepared by Jaye S. Niefeld, executive vice president of Bozell, Inc., an advertising agency. Inquiries or requests for diskettes should be addressed to: Bozell, Inc., International Division, 40 West 23rd Street, New York, N.Y. 10010

A. Target Country Data: France
   1. General
      *a.* Capital: Paris
      *b.* Population: 55.8 million (1988)
      *c.* Ten largest cities:

| | |
|---|---|
| Paris | 2,176,243 |
| (+ 6 suburbs) | 7,008,000 |
| Lyon | 1,220,884 |
| Marseilles | 1,110,511 |
| Lille | 936,295 |
| Bordeaux | 640,012 |
| Toulouse | 541,271 |
| Nantes | 464,857 |
| Nice | 449,496 |
| Toulon | 410,293 |
| Grenoble | 393,021 |

      *d.* Area: 543,965 sq. km.
      *e.* Official language: French
   2. Political
      *a.* Head of state: François Mitterand (1981)
      *b.* Head of government: Prime Minister Michel Rocard
      *c.* Officials:

| | |
|---|---|
| Henri Nallet | Agriculture |
| Jack Lang | Culture |
| Jean-Pierre Chevenement | Defense |
| Jacques Pelletier | Development cooperation |
| Pierre Beregovoy | Economy finance budget |
| Lionel Jospin | Education |
| Roland Dumas | Foreign affairs |
| Roger Fauroux | Industry foreign trade |
| Pierre Joxe | Interior |
| Pierre Arpaillange | Justice |

      *d.* Administrative subdivisions: 22 regional economic districts, 95 departments (metropolitan France).
      *e.* Legislature: Bicameral parliament; 577-member National Assembly and 292-member Senate. In the Assembly: Socialist Party (PS) and allies, 275; Rally for the Republic (RPR), 130; Union for French Democracy (UDF), 90; Union of Centrists (UDC), 41; Communist Party (PCF), 27; National Front (FN), 1; independents, 13.
      *f.* Elections: Presidential elections are held every seven years; last, May 8, 1988; next, scheduled May 1995. Senate members serve nine-year terms; one-third elected every three years; next, scheduled September 1989. Assem-

bly members are elected for five-year terms. Last, June 1988; next, by June 1993.

(For an assessment of political stability and risk, refer to the latest volume of Frost & Sullivan: Country Forecasts).

3. Commercial
   *a.* Sectors of government participation: Communications, transportation, utilities, energy, insurance and banking, petrochemicals, aerospace, steel, aluminum, textiles, armaments, electronics.
   *b.* Currency exchange system: Cooperative intervention within the European Monetary System.
   *c.* Exchange rate: March 1, 1989: 1 franc = $ 0.1576.
   *d.* French commercial attaché (in England): c/o Consulate General of France, 24 Rutland Gate, London SW 7, England.
   *f.* BOZELL office in France: SYNERGIE/BOZELL, 59, Boulevard Exelmans, 75016 Paris, France, Tel: 47 43 30 00, André Gohet, managing director.

4. *Economic indicators*

| | *1985* | *1986* | *1987* | *1988* |
|---|---|---|---|---|
| *a.* Production, inflation, growth | | | | |
| GDP ($bn) | 522.25 | 724.63 | 880.00 | e919.60 |
| Per capita ($) | 9,465 | 13,080 | 15,830 | e16,480 |
| Real growth rate (%) | 1.7 | 2.1 | 2.2 | e2.5 |
| Inflation rate (%) | 5.8 | 2.5 | 3.1 | e2.5 |
| Capital investment ($bn) | 99.37 | 137.13 | 141.11 | e147.10 |
| Budget balance ($bn) | −15.68 | −18.09 | e−17.62 | e−27.58 |
| *b.* Labor | | | | |
| Change in real wages (%) | .3 | 2.0 | 1.4 | - |
| Unemployment rate (%) | 10.3 | 10.7 | 10.4 | e11.3 |
| *c.* International | | | | |
| Debt service ratio (%) | 6.4 | - | - | - |
| Current account ($bn) | − .04 | 3.00 | −4.40 | e−4.00 |
| Exports ($bn) | 95.93 | 117.99 | 148.30 | e156.00 |
| Imports ($bn) | 101.20 | 120.34 | 160.30 | e166.25 |
| Currency change (%) | 11.7 | 4.9 | 4.1 | e−3.6 |

e = Estimate.

   *d.* Principal imports: machinery, automobiles, chemicals, textiles, iron and steel, and agricultural products; mainly from West Germany, Italy, Belgium, and the United Kingdom.

*e.* Principal exports: machinery, iron and steel, petroleum, chemicals, and food; mainly to West Germany, Italy, Belgium, and the United States.

5. Social indicators (1988 estimates)

*a.* Population

| | |
|---|---|
| Annual growth (%) | 0.4% |
| Infant deaths per thousand | 8 |
| Under 15 | 20% |
| 15–24 | NA |
| 25–34 | NA |
| 35–44 | NA |
| 45–55 | NA |
| 55 and over | NA |
| Urban population (%) | 73% |
| Urban growth (%) | 1% |
| Literacy (%) | 99% |

*b.* Work force distribution

| | |
|---|---|
| Agriculture (%) | 8% |
| Industry-commerce (%) | 45% |
| Services (%) | 46% |
| Union (%) | 20% |

*c.* Ethnic groups: European, African, others

*d.* Languages: French

*e.* Religions: Roman Catholic (90%), Protestants, Jews, Moslems

B. Market Profile

1. The product category in the France

*a.* Brief history:

(1) When introduced: ____________________

____________________

(2) Percent penetration: ____________________

____________________

(3) Outlook: ____________________

____________________

(4) Major competitors: ____________________

____________________

(5) Role of imports: ____________________

____________________

(6) Technology outlook: ____________________

____________________

(7) Traditional distribution channels: ____________________

____________________

(8) Nontraditional channels: ____________________

____________________

(9) Expected impact of EEC legislation ______________

______________________________

*b.* Descriptions of our brand and French competitors:

| *Attribute* | *Our Brand* (yes/no) | *French* *Brand A* (yes/no) | *Brand B* (yes/no) | *Brand C* (yes/no) |
|---|---|---|---|---|
| Features: | | | | |
| (1) ______ | ______ | ______ | ______ | ______ |
| (2) ______ | ______ | ______ | ______ | ______ |
| (3) ______ | ______ | ______ | ______ | ______ |
| (4) ______ | ______ | ______ | ______ | ______ |
| (5) ______ | ______ | ______ | ______ | ______ |

Recommended changes in our brand's features:
(1) ______________________________
(2) ______________________________
(3) ______________________________

| | | | | |
|---|---|---|---|---|
| Sizes: | | | | |
| (1) ______ | ______ | ______ | ______ | ______ |
| (2) ______ | ______ | ______ | ______ | ______ |
| (3) ______ | ______ | ______ | ______ | ______ |
| (4) ______ | ______ | ______ | ______ | ______ |
| (5) ______ | ______ | ______ | ______ | ______ |

Recommended changes in our brand's sizes:
(1) ______________________________
(2) ______________________________
(3) ______________________________

| | | | | |
|---|---|---|---|---|
| Packaging: | | | | |
| (1) ______ | ______ | ______ | ______ | ______ |
| (2) ______ | ______ | ______ | ______ | ______ |
| (3) ______ | ______ | ______ | ______ | ______ |
| (4) ______ | ______ | ______ | ______ | ______ |
| (5) ______ | ______ | ______ | ______ | ______ |

Recommended changes in our brand's packaging:
(1) ______________________________
(2) ______________________________
(3) ______________________________

| | | | | |
|---|---|---|---|---|
| Price: | | | | |
| (1) ______ | ______ | ______ | ______ | ______ |
| (2) ______ | ______ | ______ | ______ | ______ |
| (3) ______ | ______ | ______ | ______ | ______ |
| (4) ______ | ______ | ______ | ______ | ______ |
| (5) ______ | ______ | ______ | ______ | ______ |

Recommended target country prices for our brand:
(1) ______________________________
(2) ______________________________
(3) ______________________________

Other:
(1) ______ ______ ______ ______ ______
(2) ______ ______ ______ ______ ______
(3) ______ ______ ______ ______ ______
(4) ______ ______ ______ ______ ______
(5) ______ ______ ______ ______ ______

Recommended changes:
(1) ____________________________________
(2) ____________________________________
(3) ____________________________________

*c.* Category's position in the product life cycle within France:

___ (1) Introductory stage
___ (2) Early stage of development
___ (3) Beginning of mature stage
___ (4) Middle of mature stage
___ (5) End of mature stage
___ (6) Declining stage

2. The marketplace

*a.* Sales history of important competitive brands in France.

| | *Number of Units* | | | | | | | |
|---|---|---|---|---|---|---|---|---|
| *Competitive Brand* | *1985* | *% Inc.* | *1986* | *% Inc.* | *1987* | *% Inc.* | *1988* | *% Inc.* |
| ______ | ___ | ___% | ___ | ___% | ___ | ___% | ___ | ___% |
| ______ | ___ | ___ | ___ | ___ | ___ | ___ | ___ | ___ |
| ______ | ___ | ___ | ___ | ___ | ___ | ___ | ___ | ___ |
| ______ | ___ | ___ | ___ | ___ | ___ | ___ | ___ | ___ |
| ______ | ___ | ___ | ___ | ___ | ___ | ___ | ___ | ___ |

| | | | *In Monetary Units* | | | | | |
|---|---|---|---|---|---|---|---|---|
| *Competitive Brand* | *1985* | *% Inc.* | *1986* | *% Inc.* | *1987* | *% Inc.* | *1988* | *% Inc.* |
| ______ | ___ | ___% | ___ | ___% | ___ | ___% | ___ | ___% |
| ______ | ___ | ___ | ___ | ___ | ___ | ___ | ___ | ___ |
| ______ | ___ | ___ | ___ | ___ | ___ | ___ | ___ | ___ |
| ______ | ___ | ___ | ___ | ___ | ___ | ___ | ___ | ___ |
| ______ | ___ | ___ | ___ | ___ | ___ | ___ | ___ | ___ |

3. Distribution in France

*a.* Key channels:

____________________________________
____________________________________
____________________________________
____________________________________
____________________________________

*b.* Sell-in practices:

*c.* Trade advertising (including co-op):

*d.* Trade's buying dynamics:

*e.* Typical service and support practices in France:

*f.* Potential distribution companies in France:

(1) ____________
(2) ____________
(3) ____________
(4) ____________
(5) ____________

*g.* If no appropriate distribution companies are available practical, these companies are alternatives to distribu our brand:

4. **Advertising and promotion for major French competitors**

*a.* **Expenditures, by medium:**

| *Consumer Media* | *Monetary Amount for Each Brand* | | | |
|---|---|---|---|---|
| | *Brand A* | *Brand B* | *Brand C* | *Brand D* |
| TV | ____ | ____ | ____ | ____ |
| Radio | ____ | ____ | ____ | ____ |
| Newspaper | ____ | ____ | ____ | ____ |
| Magazines | ____ | ____ | ____ | ____ |
| Other | | | | |
| Co-op | ____ | ____ | ____ | ____ |
| Direct | ____ | ____ | ____ | ____ |
| Total Consumer Advertising | ____ | ____ | ____ | ____ |
| *Trade Media* | | | | |
| TV | ____ | ____ | ____ | ____ |
| Radio | ____ | ____ | ____ | ____ |
| Newspaper | ____ | ____ | ____ | ____ |
| Magazines | ____ | ____ | ____ | ____ |
| Other | ____ | ____ | ____ | ____ |
| Total Trade Advertising | ____ | ____ | ____ | ____ |
| *Promotional Activities* | *Yes/No* | *Yes/No* | *Yes/No* | *Yes/No* |
| Sales brochures | ____ | ____ | ____ | ____ |
| Product specification sheets | ____ | ____ | ____ | ____ |
| Displays | ____ | ____ | ____ | ____ |
| Product demonstrations | ____ | ____ | ____ | ____ |
| Market research | ____ | ____ | ____ | ____ |

*b.* **Share of Voice Compared with Share of Market:**

| *Brand* | *Share-of-Voice* | *Share-of-Market* |
|---|---|---|
| ____ | ____% | ____% |
| ____ | ____% | ____% |
| ____ | ____% | ____% |

*c.* **Analysis of Creative and Media Strategies for Past Three Years (Target Country Competition):**

| *Creative Positioning* | *French* | | |
|---|---|---|---|
| | *Brand A* (Yes/No) | *Brand B* (Yes/No) | *Brand C* (Yes/No) |
| (1) ____ | ____ | ____ | ____ |
| (2) ____ | ____ | ____ | ____ |

(3) ______________ ________ ________ ________
(4) ______________ ________ ________ ________
(5) ______________ ________ ________ ________

| Media Strategies | Brand A (Yes/No) | Brand B (Yes/No) | Brand C (Yes/No) |
|---|---|---|---|
| (1) ______________ | ________ | ________ | ________ |
| (2) ______________ | ________ | ________ | ________ |
| (3) ______________ | ________ | ________ | ________ |
| (4) ______________ | ________ | ________ | ________ |
| (5) ______________ | ________ | ________ | ________ |

*d.* Examples of Competitors' Advertising Compared with Our Brand's Domestic Advertising:

5. The consumer

*a.* Define the Heavy User As Well As the *Marketable Segments** That Will Account for Sales:

______________________________________________
______________________________________________
______________________________________________
______________________________________________

**Marketable segment* refers to descriptors of our target group that go beyond the usual demographics. These descriptors should let us know what is unique about the people we are trying to reach. For example, it is not enough to say "women 18 to 49." Eighteen-year-olds have little in common with 49-year-olds. We need to know the *specific attributes* that differentiate certain groups of users. Which attribute—whether demographic, psychographic, life-style, etc.—makes this segment "marketable."

*b.* Attitudes/Motivations, Particularly of Heavy Users. Cultural Differences from Domestic Users:

______________________________________________
______________________________________________
______________________________________________
______________________________________________

*c.* Behavior Patterns. Differences from Domestic Users.

______________________________________________
______________________________________________
______________________________________________
______________________________________________

6. Strategic research findings

*a.* Competitor *positionings* in target country. Include gaps in positionings.

| Positioning* | French Brand A (major/ minor) | French Brand B (major/ minor) | French Brand C (major/ minor) |
|---|---|---|---|
| (1) ______ | ______ | ______ | ______ |
| (2) ______ | ______ | ______ | ______ |
| (3) ______ | ______ | ______ | ______ |
| (4) ______ | ______ | ______ | ______ |
| (5) ______ | ______ | ______ | ______ |
| (6) ______ | ______ | ______ | ______ |
| (7) ______ | ______ | ______ | ______ |
| (8) ______ | ______ | ______ | ______ |
| (9) ______ | ______ | ______ | ______ |

*Indicate whether the position is used in a *major* way, a *minor* way, or not used at all by the competition.

*b.* Potential positionings not now being used in a major way by French competitors:

| *Positioning Not Used* | *Potential Effectiveness (Rate 1 through 5, 5 = Most Effective)* |
|---|---|
| (1) ______ | ______ |
| (2) ______ | ______ |
| (3) ______ | ______ |
| (4) ______ | ______ |
| (5) ______ | ______ |

*c.* Key consumer benefits being filled by the product:
(1) ______
(2) ______
(3) ______
(4) ______
(5) ______

*d.* The importance of brand attributes/features (rank in order of importance):
(1) ______
(2) ______
(3) ______
(4) ______
(5) ______

*e.* Needed alterations in our brand to create a competitive edge:
(1) ______
(2) ______

(3) ______________________________
(4) ______________________________
(5) ______________________________

*f.* Perceived brand and French competitors' *strengths*:

| *Strengths* | *Our Brand* (yes/no) | French *Brand A* (yes/no) | French *Brand B* (yes/no) | French *Brand C* (yes/no) |
|---|---|---|---|---|
| Product features: | | | | |
| (1) ________ | ______ | ______ | ______ | |
| (2) ________ | ______ | ______ | ______ | |
| (3) ________ | ______ | ______ | ______ | |
| Distribution: | | | | |
| (1) ________ | ______ | ______ | ______ | |
| (2) ________ | ______ | ______ | ______ | |
| (3) ________ | ______ | ______ | ______ | |
| Marketing activities: | | | | |
| (1) ________ | ______ | ______ | ______ | |
| (2) ________ | ______ | ______ | ______ | |
| (3) ________ | ______ | ______ | ______ | |

*g.* Perceived brand and competitor *weaknesses*:

| *Weaknesses* | *Our Brand* (yes/no) | French *Brand A* (yes/no) | French *Brand B* (yes/no) | French *Brand C* (yes/no) |
|---|---|---|---|---|
| Product features: | | | | |
| (1) ________ | ______ | ______ | ______ | |
| (2) ________ | ______ | ______ | ______ | |
| (3) ________ | ______ | ______ | ______ | |
| Distribution: | | | | |
| (1) ________ | ______ | ______ | ______ | |
| (2) ________ | ______ | ______ | ______ | |
| (3) ________ | ______ | ______ | ______ | |
| Marketing activities: | | | | |
| (1) ________ | ______ | ______ | ______ | |
| (2) ________ | ______ | ______ | ______ | |
| (3) ________ | ______ | ______ | ______ | |

C. Problems and Opportunities

1. Problems

*a.* ______________________________
*b.* ______________________________
*c.* ______________________________
*d.* ______________________________
*e.* ______________________________
*f.* ______________________________

2. Opportunities
   *a.* ______________________________
   *b.* ______________________________
   *c.* ______________________________
   *d.* ______________________________
   *e.* ______________________________
   *f.* ______________________________

D. Objectives

1. *Marketing objectives*
   *a.* Unit sales objectives:

| 1992 | 1993 | 1994 | 1995 | 1996 |
|---|---|---|---|---|

   *b.* Monetary sales objectives:

| 1992 | 1993 | 1994 | 1995 | 1996 |
|---|---|---|---|---|

   *c.* Market share objectives:

| 1992 | 1993 | 1994 | 1995 | 1996 |
|---|---|---|---|---|

   *d.* Profit objectives:

| 1992 | 1993 | 1994 | 1995 | 1996 |
|---|---|---|---|---|

Projected Operating Statement

| | *1992* | *1993* | *1994* | *1995* | *1996* |
|---|---|---|---|---|---|
| Turnover | ____ | ____ | ____ | ____ | ____ |
| Cost of goods | ____ | ____ | ____ | ____ | ____ |
| Gross margin | ____ | ____ | ____ | ____ | ____ |
| Gross margin % | ___% | ___% | ___% | ___% | ___% |

| | | | | | |
|---|---|---|---|---|---|
| Other costs: | | | | | |
| 1. Sales | ___ | ___ | ___ | ___ | ___ |
| 2. Advertising | ___ | ___ | ___ | ___ | ___ |
| 3. Administration | ___ | ___ | ___ | ___ | ___ |
| 4. Service | ___ | ___ | ___ | ___ | ___ |
| 5. Freight | ___ | ___ | ___ | ___ | ___ |
| 6. Legal | ___ | ___ | ___ | ___ | ___ |
| 7. Other | ___ | ___ | ___ | ___ | ___ |
| Total other costs | ___ | ___ | ___ | ___ | ___ |
| Percentage other costs | | | | | |
| Pretax profit | | | | | |
| Percentage pretax profit | | | | | |
| Taxes | ___ | ___ | ___ | ___ | ___ |
| After-tax profit | | | | | |
| Percentage after-tax profit | ___ | ___ | ___ | ___ | ___ |

2. Creative objectives
   *a.* Awareness:

   *b.* Emotional response:

   *c.* Perception (beliefs, images):

   *d.* Acceptance (changes in attitudes, preferences):

   *e.* Overt behavior (intent to buy, brand switching, etc.):

3. Media objectives
   *a.* Exposure of target groups (reach):

   *b.* Frequency of exposure:

   *c.* Comparison with anticipated competitive media activity:

   *d.* Impact by means of special media events:

*e.* Pan-European media; French national media; or only specified cities within France.

4. Promotion objectives
   *a.* Increase traffic/generate leads:

   *b.* Encourage sampling/information inquiries:

   *c.* Enhance distribution:

E. Strategy Development
1. Marketing strategies
   *a.* Anticipated source of sales (where will sales come from—competitors? expanded category? other?):

   *b.* Marketable segment (see page 162 for definition):

   *c.* Marketing focus:
   (1) Product features

   (2) Pricing/discounting

   (3) Distribution

   (4) Service

(5) Advertising/promotion

______________________________

______________________________

2. Consumer creative strategies
   *a.* Select the *crucial attribute*, based on a market position that is currently "unoccupied" or one that would put our brand head-to-head against one or more competitors:

   ______________________________

   ______________________________

   ______________________________

   ______________________________

   ______________________________

   *b.* Tonality:

   ______________________________

   ______________________________

   ______________________________

   ______________________________

   ______________________________

   *c.* Relevant images:

   ______________________________

   ______________________________

   ______________________________

   ______________________________

   ______________________________

3. Trade creative strategies
   *a.* Who we are:

   ______________________________

   ______________________________

   *b.* Our product advantages to the trade:

   ______________________________

   ______________________________

   *c.* Our product advantages to consumers:

   ______________________________

   ______________________________

   *d.* How the trade can become part of our distribution system:

   ______________________________

   ______________________________

4. Consumer media strategies
   *a.* Media relevance:

   ______________________________

   ______________________________

   ______________________________

*b.* Impact media or event media potential:

______________________________

______________________________

______________________________

*c.* Consumer media budget:

______________________________

5. Trade media strategies:

*a.* Media relevance:

______________________________

______________________________

______________________________

*b.* Impact media or trade event media potential:

______________________________

______________________________

______________________________

*c.* Trade media budget:

______________________________

Some typical media costs and efficiencies:

| *Daily Newspapers* | | *Circulation* | *Audience (000)* | *Cost per B/W Page* |
|---|---|---|---|---|
| *Le Figaro* | | 405,678 | 1,296 | 295,000 F |
| *Le Monde* | | 290,212 | 1,056 | 185,000 |
| *Libération* | | 146,846 | 750 | 69,000 |
| *Les Echos* | | 72 731 | | 90,000 |
| *Weekly News Magazines* | | *Circulation* | *Audience (000)* | *Cost per 4/C Page* |
| *L'Express* | | 405,249 | 2,300 | 150,000 F |
| *Nouvel Observateur* | | 303,972 | 1,919 | 114,000 |
| *Le Point* | | 262,639 | 1,710 | 115,160 |
| *L'Evenement du Jeudi* | | 140,798 | 1,208 | 70,000 |
| *Weekly Illustrated Magazines* | | | | |
| *Paris Match* | | 651,941 | 4,194 | 168,500 F |
| *Figaro Magazine* | | 617,950 | 3,901 | 210,000 |
| *V.S.D.* | | 195,744 | 1,826 | 109,000 |
| *Weekly Business Magazines* | | | | |
| *L'Expansion* | | 159,744 | 940 | 104,299 F |
| *Le Nouvel Economiste* | | 92,753 | 437 | 63,000 |
| *Sport Magazines* | | | | |
| *Action Auto* | (m) | 342,554 | 2,360 | 82,000 F |
| *L'Equipe* | (w) | 254,866 | 1,327 | 101,000 |
| *Onze* | (m) | 136,108 | 1,572 | 64,000 |

| *Weekly TV Magazines* | | | |
|---|---|---|---|
| *Télé 7 Jours* | 3,145,604 | 10,532 | 289,000 F |
| *Télé Poche* | 1,740,765 | 6,892 | 160,000 |
| *Télé Star* | 1,540,128 | 5,266 | 158,700 |
| *Téléloisirs* | 1,071,371 | 3,088 | 130,000 |
| *Télérama* | 488,229 | 2,106 | 99,800 |

| *Television Channel* | *Day* | *Time* | *Audience* | *Cost* |
|---|---|---|---|---|
| T.F. 1 | Mon. | 20.30 hours | 26.6% | 420,000 F |
| | Sun. | 20.40 | 25.3 | 450,000 |
| A 2 | Tue. | 20.35 | 23.1 | 386,600 |
| | Fri. | 20.35 | 17.8 | 243,700 |
| F.R. 3 (pay TV) | Mon. | 20.35 | 10.2 | 150,000 |
| | Wed. | 19.15 | 8.4 | 60,000 |
| Canal 4 | Tue. | 19.15 | 2.9 | 40,000 |
| | Mon. | 19.30 | 2.7 | 42,000 |
| La Cinq | Thu. | 20.30 | 8.1 | 93,000 |
| | Mon. | 20.30 | 8.1 | 93,000 |
| M 6 | Thu. | 20.30 | 5.3 | 70,000 |
| | Tue. | 20.15 | 4.2 | 60,000 |

| *Radio* | *Time* | *Audience* | *Cost* | | |
|---|---|---|---|---|---|
| | | (000) | *Weekday* | *Fri.* | *Sat.* |
| R.T.L. | 11.00/13.00 | 3,788 | 32,000F | 37,000F | 30,000F |
| | 8.30/10.00 | 2,941 | 24,000 | 28,000 | 43,500 |
| Europe | 6.30/ 8.30 | 4,330 | 44,000 | 49,500 | 14,500 |
| | 8.30/10.00 | 2,354 | 44,000 | 49,500 | 26,500 |
| R.M.C. | 7.00/ 8.30 | 1,502 | 17,000 | 19,500 | 13,000 |
| | 8.30/11.30 | 1,004 | 13,000 | 15,000 | 14,200 |
| Sud Radio | 7.00/ 8.30 | 244 | 5,600 | 6,440 | 3,000 |
| | 8.30/11.00 | 179 | 4,000 | 4,600 | 3,600 |

*d.* Special considerations (seasonality, regionality, etc.):

______________________________________

______________________________________

______________________________________

______________________________________

______________________________________

6. Promotion strategies

*a.* Trade advertising:

______________________________________

______________________________________

*b.* Displays:

*c.* Co-op advertising:

*d.* Couponing/sampling:

*e.* Premiums:

*f.* Sales brochures:

*g.* Technical specification sheets:

*h.* Telemarketing:

*i.* Direct marketing:

7. Service strategies

*a.* Training program for sales and service personnel:

*b.* Training manuals in target country language:

*c.* User instructions in target country language:

*d.* Establishment or licensing of service centers:

*e.* Warehousing of product and parts:

*f.* Computer ordering:

*g.* Warranty program: ______________________________

______________________________

8. Financing strategies
   *a.* ______________________________
   *b.* ______________________________
   *c.* ______________________________
   *d.* ______________________________
   *e.* ______________________________
9. Distribution strategies
   *a.* ______________________________
   *b.* ______________________________
   *c.* ______________________________
10. Research strategies
    *a.* Track brand shares.
    *b.* Assess consumer satisfaction and dissatisfaction with our brand.
    *c.* Determine the degree to which we have successfully tapped into the target country culture.
    *d.* Measure advertising effectiveness.
    *e.* Measure distribution effectiveness.
    *f.* Other.

F. Restrictions applicable to advertising in France (for details, refer to European Association of Advertising Agencies: Laws and Regulations on Advertising in Europe. 28, avenue du Barbeau; B-1160 Brussels, Belgium). A summary of 1992 legislation is available for each EEC country.

1. Media
   *a.* Media availability and restrictions.

| | *Permitted* | *Prohibited* | *Restricted* |
|---|---|---|---|
| Television* | X | | |
| Radio | X | | |
| Cinema | X | | |
| Newspapers† | X | | |
| Magazines | X | | |
| Outdoor‡ | | | X |

**TV*: Restrictions on As for 3- and 8-second commercials. One brand can be advertised in a maximum of two commercials of 3 seconds per day and these commercials must be in different blocks.

†*Newspapers*: Newspapers can refuse advertisements if these are not suitable or are contrary to the general policy of the newspaper, or if they might provoke protests from readers.

‡*Outdoor*: Maximum height for posters is 750 cm from the ground. They must not block windows. Poster sizes decrease according to the size of the cities where they are located.

*b.* New media.

Teletext: The French teletext system ANTIOPE only allows advertising on its private TUBE network, which is displayed in some Metro stations and in shopping centers. The public ANTIOPE TV channel, available by means of a decoder, or in the morning on FR3, does not offer advertising.

Videotex: Minitel and videotapes for home viewing accept advertising.

| | Permitted | Prohibited | Restricted |
|---|---|---|---|
| Sponsorship. | X | | |
| Point-of-sale. | X | | |
| Sales promotion. | | | X |

These are subject to legislation (decree 77–105P) and can only be organized for the products available during the promotion time and with the same price conditions.

2. Products—General conditions, legislation, media restrictions, and voluntary guidelines are available for the following product categories:
   *a.* Alcoholic beverages.
   *b.* Household cleaning products.
   *c.* Cosmetics and personal hygiene.
   *d.* Food.
   *e.* Medicinal and o.t.c. products, treatments.
   *f.* Tobacco.
   *g.* Other.
3. Services—General conditions, legislation, media restrictions, and voluntary guidelines are available for the following services categories:
   *a.* Financial.
   *b.* Insurance.
   *c.* Loans, credit, mortgages.
   *d.* Medical professions.
   *e.* Other.
4. General advertising restrictions
   *a.* Betting, games and lotteries, gifts, premiums, competitions, and sweepstakes

      *Restricted by law on:*
      Television
      Radio
      Cinema
      Newspapers
      Magazines
      Outdoor
      Point-of-sale
      Sales promotion
      Packaging/labelling

Sponsorship
New media

*b.* **Advertising to children.**
*Restricted by voluntary guidelines on:*
Television*
Radio*
Cinema*
Newspapers*
Magazines*
Outdoor*
Point-of-sale*
Sales promotion
Packaging/labelling
Sponsorship
New media

*Children may not be used as endorsers for a product or service.

Children may be used as presenters for noncontroversial products and services connected with children when they are shown together with adults.

Cartoons and celebrities are prohibited in advertisements directed to children.

*c.* **Guarantees.**
*Restricted by law and by voluntary guidelines on:*
Television*
Radio*
Cinema*
Newspapers*
Magazines*
Outdoor*
Point-of-sale*
Sales promotion*
Packaging/labelling
Sponsorship
New media

All media subject to voluntary guidelines.

Advertising that refers to a report by an expert must indicate the qualifications of the expert.

*d.* **Mail-order advertising.**
*Restricted by law and by voluntary guidelines on:*
Television*
Radio*
Cinema*
Newspapers*
Magazines*
Outdoor*
Point-of-sale*
Sales promotion*
Packaging/labelling
Sponsorship
New media

In addition to the legal requirements, direct mail must show any material that permits the recipient to identify the firm, and in particular its name and address.

It is prohibited to send unsolicited articles that must be paid for by the recipient.

### *e.* Political, religious advertising or advertising with political or religious content.

*Restricted by law and by voluntary guidelines (all) on:*
Television
Radio
Cinema
Newspapers
Magazines
Outdoor
Point-of-sale
Sales promotion
Packaging/labelling
Sponsorship
New media

Commercials that cast a slur on the reputation of the government, the nation, or high officials are prohibited.

### *f.* Pornography, sexism.

*Restricted by law and by voluntary guidelines (all) on:*
Television
Radio
Cinema
Newspapers
Magazines
Outdoor
Point-of-sale
Sales promotion
Packaging/labelling
Sponsorship
New media

All pornographic commercials and commercials for pornography must be approved by the Control Commission.

Only advertising limited to the title of the film is permitted. No frivolous or aggressive advertising.

Advertising for films prohibited to children and adolescents must have the approval of the Control Commission. The industry observes voluntary restrictions and agrees to keep promotion for pornographic films acceptable to all audiences outside the appropriate cinemas.

Commericals depicting women in the role of housewives only or depicting men and women in degrading situations are prohibited.

Service providers on Minitel (Videotex) are considered to be promoting immoral activities and are required to pay an additional premium.

### *g.* Testimonials, endorsements.

*Governed by law and by voluntary guidelines on:*
Television*
Radio*

Cinema*
Newspapers*
Magazines*
Outdoor*
Point-of-sale*
Sales promotion*
Packaging/labelling
Sponsorship
New media

*Endorsements for the following products and services are prohibited by law: tobacco, alcohol, investments and savings, cartoon advertising to children.

In addition to these prohibitions, French advertisers voluntarily observe the recommendations of the I.C.C. code.

### *h.* Vocabulary, language.

*Restricted by law and by C.N.C.L. guidelines (all) on:*
Television
Radio
Cinema
Newspapers
Magazines
Outdoor
Point-of-sale
Sales promotion
Packaging/labelling
Sponsorship
New media

French commercials must avoid the use of foreign-language terms. Foreign-language print advertisements are totally prohibited in local media.

Commercials cannot address the consumer by the familiar "tu." The use of the following words or their substitutes is restricted: happiness, the first, the best, the only one, exclusive, exceptional, unique, natural, pure, healthy, real, authentic, fresh, new.

### *i.* Road Safety

*Restricted by voluntary guidelines on:*
Television
Radio
Cinema
Newspapers
Magazines
Outdoor
Point-of-sale
Sales promotion
Packaging/labelling
Sponsorship
New media

### *j.* Other Important Restrictions:

Voluntary media guidelines also restrict commercials with respect to the following:

The presentation of social groups.
The presentation of new products.
Misleading advertising.
Enhancing situations of unfair competition.
Comparative advertising is prohibited.

G. Prototype Outline of Communications Plan for MultiNational EEC Brand

1. Situation analysis
   *a.* Brief summary statement of the category's performance in the target country.
   *b.* Share trends of competitive brands.
   *c.* Volume trends of competitive brands.
2. Financial forecasts
   *a.* Brief summary of brand's projected financial picture—1992 and forward.
   *b.* Brand's projected P&L—1992 and forward.
3. Marketing plan
   *a.* Statement of brand's consumer and trade marketing objectives.
   *b.* Statement of brand's consumer and trade marketing strategies—how the objectives will be achieved.
   *c.* Marketing rationale—support for strategies.
4. Advertising plan
   *a.* Statement of brand's consumer and trade advertising objectives.
   *b.* Statement of brand's consumer and trade advertising strategies.
   *c.* Advertising rationale—support for strategies.
   *d.* Creative exhibits.
   *e.* Itemized creative budget.
5. Media plan
   *a.* Consumer and trade media objectives.
   *b.* Consumer and trade media strategies.
   *c.* Media rationale.
   *d.* Itemized media budget.
6. Sales promotion plan
   *a.* Objectives.
   *b.* Strategies.
   *c.* Sales promotion rationale.
   *d.* Itemized sales promotion budget.
7. Appendix
   (Supporting data)

# CHAPTER 16

# OUR SECRET WEAPON

## or "MAYBE YOU KNOW MY COUSIN IN TOLEDO"

As this book comes to a close, if you have any remaining doubts about how to succeed overseas, I urge you *not* to dwell on trade balances, cheaper overseas labor, the comparable strength or weakness of the dollar, or any of the following statistics people sometimes use to create fear in our hearts:

- In 1974 imported shoes represented about 18 percent of the total shoes we purchased in this country; today, the number exceeds 50 percent.
- Ten years ago 90 percent of the power tools sold in this country were made here; today over one-third of them come from overseas.
- Over half the luggage we buy in the United States comes from overseas, generally from Mexico or Taiwan.
- Over 25 percent of the cars sold here each year come from Japan, Korea, Germany, Britain, or France.

In spite of these overwhelming numbers showing the importance of overseas production, and regardless of people's attitudes that Japanese cars are better or that Italian shoes fit better or that we have become a service country, we have a few secret weapons. Sadly, the "secret" is kept here and not abroad.

## AMERICAN LIFE-STYLES ARE COPIED ALL OVER THE WORLD

A few years ago, according to a top journal in the advertising/marketing field, the following items were "in":

- Owning a BMW.
- Having a microwave oven in your kitchen.
- Running/jogging for fitness.
- White wine.
- Cordless phones.
- The Cosby Show on TV.

These "in" things might well have been in California, Connecticut, or Colorado, but the survey measured life-styles in Great Britain!

There were more "in" things:

- Natural fiber clothing.
- Burberry raincoats.
- A Harvard MBA.
- Pearl chokers.

These "in" things, these symbols of status and acceptance, were from France!

In Italy the life-style of success included eating pizza, driving a Volvo, and *English* lessons! Someone I met one time wore a Boston Celtics jacket in Rome; he had to fight people off—everyone wanted to buy it from him.

We are what we are, and our life-style and culture represent something very unique and special to most people overseas. If you can capitalize on that, you will be a successful exporter.

### What's on TV Tonight?

A recent newspaper article discussing American sports around the world indicated that our National Basketball Association games were televised in Australia, Spain, the Soviet Union, and Zimbabwe. The article added that Japan was negotiating to have two NBA teams open their next regular season in Tokyo, and that 10,000 people had attended a Julius Irving clinic in Madrid last year.

The National Football League will have two televised games in Great Britain, and there have been exhibition games at Wembley Stadium for the past few years. The NFL is also televised in Hong Kong and Iceland; two teams played an exhibition in Japan in August 1989. Over $50 million in NFL-endorsed clothing will be sold each year in Great Britain.

The National Hockey League has exhibition games in the Soviet Union and Czechoslovakia, and televised games in France, Denmark, and Sweden.

Major league baseball games are televised in Venezuela, the Dominican Republic, Mexico, and Japan.

Our culture is accepted and rapidly becoming a significant part of the rest of the world. Therein lies your opportunity to promote these acceptable themes and simply to be what you are best, American!

## America Comes to Sweden

Several years ago I arrived on a business trip in Stockholm at the same time that McDonald's opened there. My Swedish friends refused to try McDonald's, claiming they were restaurants for children.

Not too long ago, and well after that visit, one of that same group of Swedish businessmen called me in the United States. He was spending the evening in Stockholm at the company apartment since it was too late to drive home to his suburban residence. I asked him what he had been doing, and was told he had had a quick dinner at McDonald's and was going to settle down to watch "Falconcrest" on television. How quickly attitudes and tastes can change! I teased him that he was becoming an American.

## It Happens in China, Too

I visited the People's Republic of China shortly after we sold a bakery concern there a very high capacity hamburger bun-baking machine. One member of the Chinese purchasing committee had been all over the United States visiting food service companies, and we had a great deal to discuss. While most people may think of the Chinese diet as consisting of rice, fish, melons, and bread made from rice flour—anything but hamburgers and buns for the burgers—the bun-baking machine was to be installed for a fast-food restaurant in Beijing named "Donald Duck."

In the Republic of China (Taiwan), fast food used to be roadside noodle stands, oyster omelets and tea. McDonald's announced its decision to open in Taipei, the capital, and the great debate began. People feared McDonald's would change the eating habits of the people, literally eliminating rice from their diets! When the first outlet opened, it set a worldwide record for business and weekly revenues in its second week! Taiwan also has Shakey's Pizza, Baskin Robbins, Swenson's Ice Cream, Kentucky Fried Chicken, and Wendy's.

## We Are Everywhere

You can find Baskin Robbins, McDonald's, Dunkin' Donuts, and heaven knows what else in Japan. There have been times when I thought Coca-Cola was a universal word. Swenson's sells ice cream in Singapore, McDonald's sells hamburgers in France, Germany, Sweden, and Australia—you name it. The Marlboro man rides everywhere!

While some people may consider these businesses to be the worst of American culture, such products are one part of our "secret weapon." They reflect and reinforce a very specific part of American culture abroad, and the local residents in the countries where these establishments exist patronize them in great numbers. It used to be a standing joke that the only American things seen abroad were our airplanes, operated by virtually every free world airline, and rock music. Fortunately, things have improved a bit.

## Need More Assurance?

F. Scott Fitzgerald's novel *Tender Is the Night* was a best-seller in France in 1985. Kodak sells more film in China than it does in

Hong Kong. Wear a Boston Celtics warm-up jacket on the streets of Italy, and see how long it will take before people ask if you will sell it to them.

American business and America's presence are not dead overseas, but our sales representatives may be asleep, and we have begun to believe two things:

1. The other guy can do it for less.
2. No one wants American goods.

For some unknown reason, we seem to have given up on ourselves in our manufacturing and selling skills. We have relinquished ingenuity and creativity to others, and we have convinced ourselves that the stockholders' interests in our companies are best served when we produce abroad for sale here.

## We Invented It, Let's Build It!

No one in Korea or Finland was named Robert Fulton, and Fulton's steamboat sailed first in this country. So why do we allow others to dominate us in ship building? Henry Ford created the mass production line for autos in Detroit, not in Japan or Korea.

The United States is absolutely first-rate in the fast food and food service business. We are also preeminent in aircraft development and production, and the point is obvious: no one of us should ever find excuses for our products, our production, and our distribution if we have paid attention to the details and have kept ourselves not only up-to-date but aware that we always have to improve.

## We Have an Even Better Weapon, Too

All over the world, wherever I traveled, people made the same comment to me: "I have a cousin in Chicago"—or New York or wherever. This is the only country in the world that has so long a history of worldwide immigration. We are truly a melting pot where there is no such thing as an authentic American name—even the Indians migrated here from across the Bering Strait.

It has been estimated that somewhere in excess of 40 million people have emigrated from abroad to this country over the span of our national existence. While a great many of us think that all Americans speak American, the fact of the matter is that this polyglot country represents an experience quite unique in the history of humanity on this planet.

This special culture gives assurances to people everywhere that America is different and special. Swedish visitors with me in Chicago one time met a long-lost cousin in the men's room of a restaurant. Two Germans I took to a German restaurant in Chicago were astounded when the owner told them he had been only a waiter in Germany, but "here I can own the business!" We can show Finns buildings designed by Saarinen, their famous architect, and we can look at buildings designed by I. M. Pei, a Chinese.

## Closer to Home

An Italian coffee salesman came to Chicago 30 years ago with his family and a dream. He bought a small neighborhood bakery that today produces over 500,000 pounds of French and Italian bread every week for Chicago supermarkets. I recently met a young Pole who came here 12 years ago with $20 supplied by his aunt. Today he owns a $13 million machine tool business. There are relatives of these people in Italy and Poland who are still talking about this country and the opportunity it gave these newer immigrants. This is a very positive influence and aid for each of us everywhere we go.

This is America, land of people's dreams, and there are literally millions of buyers abroad who want to touch a bit of that dream by dealing with you as an American and by buying what you produce. In great measure we owe our strength and our potential to the ties that bind us to other cultures: our immigrants, each and every one of us or our ancestors.

## A Little History Lesson

In the early 19th century our immigration was primarily British and Irish. In the 1830s and '40s, German immigration began, and the greatest influx of Germans took place at the end of the 19th century. Scandinavians began coming to the United States in large numbers at about the same time as the Germans, and within 20 years of that period Italians were flocking to our shores. What a great potential and a great blend of cultures and ideas would come from these groups!

Eastern Europeans began to emigrate in great numbers into this country at the turn of the century. When the 20th century began, over three-quarters of a million eastern Europeans had already arrived. Asians began coming at the same time; then their numbers fell off a bit until the 1970s and the Vietnam War.

Latin Americans moved north initially in the 1920s in large numbers. Then their immigration really grew in the 1950s and 1960s, thanks, in part to Cuba. The American population was equally blended with one major group whose members sadly came against their will, but Africans have also been arriving as full-fledged immigrants, of their own free will, since the early 20th century.

In all, 643,000 immigrants were granted legal permanent resident status in the United States in the year ending September 30, 1988. Of those, 43 percent were from Latin America, 41 percent were from Asia, and only 10 percent were from Europe. The balance were from Africa and elsewhere. While the shift in ethnic immigration continues to alter the culture inputs of this country, that influx also continues to give us a great advantage over virtually every other country on this early because we represent something of everybody.

As an aside, since most immigrants come from Mexico and Asia, California has become the state of intended residence for most of them, with 29 percent saying that was where they wanted to live. New York is second, followed by Florida, and then by Texas.

## Yet We Forget

Many Americans have seemingly lost track or don't want to be reminded of their ethnic roots. During the 1980 census, when asked to list their ancestry group, about 6 percent said "American." An additional 6 percent left that question blank. Believe it or not, with all of the immigration of the recent past, 97 percent of us and our families have been in this country for at least four generations.

## The American Miracle

There is no other country on this earth with our mix of nationalities, races, religions, beliefs, ideas, dreams, and hopes. Those people, our ancestors, came with a dream, and they left behind the vision that this country was where dreams became reality. Any wonder then that when you meet people overseas they have a relative here? You assuredly have a relative "back there" too!

## The Secret Weapon in Reality

The real secret weapon is the general acceptance of this country overseas by people of virtually any other nationality because of the immigration ties that bind us. In certain European countries, there are "guest workers" from Turkey or Greece or Spain, for example, who live on the fringe of their host country's culture, truly not accepted into the mainstream.

Everyone has their pet scapegoat as well overseas, and that tends to diffuse any real relationship power. For example, the Swedes make fun of the Finns; the Finns pick on the Lapps; the Dutch look down their noses at the Belgians; and many British like to make fun of the Irish. We do such things too, but we do them to ourselves, we hope, not to our neighbors, and that makes a difference.

## Get Ready to Be in the Culture

When you plan a business trip for the first time to Japan, go to a Japanese restaurant in this country for a few times first. Visit a Japan-American Society office if there is one near you. Stop in at a JETRO office. Learn what the food, temperament, and ideas of the country are before you go. Imagine what a preparatory school we have right here with ethnic representation from every corner of the globe.

Because of the abundant supply of ethnic restaurants, neighborhoods, churches, and social clubs in this country, you can learn something about wherever you want to go before you ever set foot on a plane. That is a benefit unique to us, and we should easily become Yankee traders who prepare and know what our customers want.

## Just Good Memories

During the recent student riots in the People's Republic of China, I was continually haunted by the memory of a young student who walked up to me in the waiting area of the Shanghai airport several years ago. "Are you an American?" he asked. "May I just sit here and talk with you about America?" I asked him where he had learned his English, and was told from the Voice of America broadcasts.

When I was growing up, my mother used to tell me stories about her grandmother and grandfather, who emigrated from Scandinavia in the 19th century. In 1976 I went to Scandinavia for the first time, realizing that it also was the first "return" for anyone in this family since those ancestors left long ago. We all have stories about our ancestors, and the people in those countries today are just as sensitive to them as we might be.

African-Americans who tour West Africa and visit the sites where slaves were detained are often brought to tears by the emotion of that experience. Yet they too are the first "return." Those connections with the past are a tragic part of our heritage, but they are still a connection that gives us a special advantage—if we wish to take it!

No one in any country in all my years of business travel abroad ever said a negative thing about this country. While politeness had a great deal to do with it, there is an identity each of those people has with this country and what it represents in terms of past migrations and mixed cultures. You can use it, but you have to be sensitive to it! Give this part of your business an extra try. The rewards are good financially, but they are even better emotionally in terms of the relationships and the knowledge you and your associates can gain.

## SUMMARY

Just as expanding sales from state to state in this country helps a business grow and expand, so too does expanding that sales potential outside the country help you develop new business with a strong future.

Just as sales might dip in Colorado when they peak in Florida, so too might sales dip in Thailand when they peak in Italy. That's the challenge and the benefit of overseas selling.

Our roots lie overseas, and new customers await us overseas, ready to ask about and deal with Americans. Be patient, and stick with these new markets through newly learned adversities. The rewards will be yours on a grander scale than you can ever imagine.

## EXPORT TERMINOLOGY YOU OUGHT TO KNOW

*Ad valorem* (according to value). Import duties are generally based on the ad valorem value of goods.

*Advance against documents.* This is a loan made against the security or collateral value of the documents that confirm a shipment and its value.

*Advising bank.* An exporter's local bank that handles letters of credit on behalf of a foreign bank. It advises the exporter when the letter of credit (L/C) has been opened, the terms of the letter, etc.

*Airway bill.* A bill of lading for air shipments which covers all flights, domestic and international. It serves as a receipt for the shipper and a document for tracing goods. There are also inland bills of lading and ocean bills of lading.

*Barter or countertrade.* This is a means of effecting a deal without cash, for example, an exchange of goods for goods, seller to buyer, where both sides feel they can optimize the deal and gain a profit. This device is often used when there is a problem obtaining dollars in an overseas market.

*Bill of lading.* A document that specifies the terms and agreements between a company and its shipper. Shippers generally offer bills of lading as supplied by carriers. Depending on how bills of lading are written, they can also act as titles to the goods.

*Bonded warehouse.* A storage facility where goods in transit can be stored without duty payment until they are picked up and/or released by the seller or the seller's bank.

*Carnet.* A document that will allow manufacturers or their agents to bring goods temporarily into a country—generally for display purposes at a show—without duty since the goods will leave the country after the show.

*Cash against documents.* A payment technique by which the buyer is obligated to remit payment on receipt and verification of the documents that generally accompany an order.

*Cash with order.* Another payment technique—cash in advance—whereby the buyer remits payment with the order. Your credit department can help establish policies on all incoming orders based on credit reports and financial information often supplied by a buyer or his bank or other sellers with whom the buyer does business.

*Certificate of inspection.* A third-party verification of the condition of goods being shipped (and even the packing materials in some instances) when such verification is required by the buyer and/or the country into which the goods are being shipped.

*Certificate of origin.* A document required by certain companies that will verify the source of manufacture. Some countries, notably those in Africa and the Caribbean, will expect a certificate of origin if the goods seem to be from South Africa, for example.

*C&F, CIF.* For an explanation of these terms, see Chapter 14.

*CDV* (current or commercial domestic value). This system is used in some countries, e.g., New Zealand, to insure that imported goods are coming in at comparable pricing relative to that expected in their home market.

*Common carrier.* Any transit company that carries your goods for profit.

*Confirmed letter of credit.* A letter of credit whose validity has been confirmed by your U.S. bank. This protects you from any possible default by the buyer or his bank since the U.S. bank, in confirming, guarantees the funds.

*Container.* A 20-foot or 40-foot self-contained shipping box. Full container rates are generally lower for shipping, and a container can be brought to your factory for loading by your own personnel through a freight forwarder. The opposite of a "container load" is, of course, "less-than-container load" or LCL.

*Countertrade.* See barter or countertrade (above).

*Drafts.* There are date drafts, sight drafts, and time drafts. These are varying types of money orders from a buyer to a seller specifying payment at a certain time, on sight of the goods or over time. Again, your credit people can help you sort these orders out to your best advantage.

*Ex.* This term is used to define pricing terms, e.g., "ex-factory" means priced at the factory door.

*Export broker/import broker.* This is an independent firm acting as intermediary to expedite shipments in or out of a country. Such brokers deal with customs, declarations, etc. and can save you a lot of hassle.

*Export license.* A document often needed to send certain goods out of the country, generally military or electronic goods. Sometimes an export license may be required for other goods as well.

*Export management company.* Although not discussed in this book, an export management company is, in effect, a manufacturer's representative that acts as the manufacturer's export department. Such a company will do all the paperwork and act as sales agent for a commission and/or fee. The largest export company in the United States is probably Getz Corporation of San Francisco. Its Japanese counterpart is probably a Japanese trading firm like Nissho-Iwai. Getz Corporation and Nissho-Iwai are also able to act as import management companies.

*FOB.* See Chapter 14.

*Force majeure.* A standard clause in all shipping contracts and in some distributor contracts which exempts that party from liability in the event certain things happen beyond their control, specifically, earthquakes, floods, typhoons, and war.

*Free port.* A designated area where goods can be moved without duty.

*Free trade zone.* An area designated as a place where goods may enter without duty for storage, display, or manufacture, and then be reexported without duty. There is a major free trade zone in Brazil.

*Freight forwarder.* A business entity available to expedite shipments by scheduling sailings, transfers, etc. for a fee.

*Import license.* A document required and issued by some governments to allow certain items to be brought into the country.

*Irrevocable letter of credit.* A letter of credit which absolutely guarantees payment if all conditions of shipment are met as agreed to and spelled out.

*Letter of credit (L/C).* A document issued by a foreign bank on instructions of the buyer, authorizing the seller to receive payment under specified terms, usually receipt of confirmed shipping documents.

*Marks.* Special letter and/or symbol indications on the outer packing cases of goods shipped to help identify them. Some buyers have a preestablished mark such as a diamond with initials inside. Other buyers might ask you to specify the mark.

*Open account.* The freest form of payment that is reserved for your best customers. They can pay on invoice within a determined payment period after the goods are shipped and possibly well after they are received; it's negotiable. Discussed in Chapter 14.

*Packing list.* A list accompanying the shipping documents that describes, in detail, what is packed in each box, and how.

*Pro-forma invoice.* A preliminary draft for buyers to give them details of the costs they will incur and the weights/sizes of their shipment before confirmation of the order. This allows customers to arrange financing and shipping plans ahead of time.

*Tare.* The weight of the containers and packing materials without the weight of the actual goods.

## FUN TERMINOLOGY YOU OUGHT TO KNOW

As I traveled, I used to wonder what word I could learn in as many different languages as possible. I wanted a word that would be universal to the extent I could also use it with taxi drivers, porters, and restaurant owners in Chicago as well as in its country of origin. Then it dawned on me that if I could learn to say "crazy" in as many languages as possible, I could have a little fun.

For whatever purpose you wish to pursue, here are the ones I remember:

*Mandarin Chinese*—fahfung (fa-foong)
*Japanese*—kichigai (kee-chee-guy)
*Pakistani Urdu*—paagel (paa-gel)
*Arabic*—majnoon (mahj-noon)
*Iranian Farsi*—divaneh (deeva-nay)
*Turkish*—deli (delli)
*Greek*—trella (trell-a)
*Spanish*—loco (loco)
*German*—verücht (fer-oocht)
*Polish*—shalona (sha-loana)
*Hebrew*—mashooga (ma-shoe-gah)
*Sweden*—tokag (too-kig)

I guarantee you laughter and surprise if you use these words here or there with the people who speak these languages. A true icebreaker for those moments when you want to bridge the gap between yourself and another person!

# THANK YOU

Experiences are made up of events *and* people. If it weren't for a great many people around the world, the business we built, and the fun we had, this book would never have come into existence, and I am grateful to every one of them.

Thank you to the following: Gunnar Grönberg and Lars Odenstrand at AutoProducts AB in Sweden; Heikki Mäki and Kari Helenius at Atoy Oy and Raimo Ahlfors in Finland; Günter Groll at Ferodo GmbH in West Germany; Bob DeWit at Continental Tire and Adrian Roggoveen in the Netherlands; Chris Boeree, Gordon Plunkett, and Alan Bond in the United Kingdom; Sil Luksich, Wynne Matthews, and Arthur Goddard at the former QH Automotive in Australia; Peter Masters at New Zealand Motor Corporation; Felix García in Puerto Rico; Richard Hands when he was in Vienna with me; Po Mar, S. K. Chung, and Eric Fung at AMF Hong Kong; Albert Lu at AMF Singapore; C. H. Lee at AMF Taiwan; Bill Brennan, Roman Rostafin, Bob Conor, and Stan Groner at the late, great AMF Incorporated; Javier Elias, Bob Bicego, and Harry Sabusawa—past and present employees of the Maremont Corporation; my "younger brother," Masao Nagata at NHK in Japan; Professor Jesus Maria Cortina of CINCO in Mexico; Mr. Huang of the All China Sports Federation in the People's Republic of China; Rafael Lecumberri, his brother, and his entire family at Agencia Llantera in Mexico; Arkadiv Cherkasov of Amtorg Trading, U.S.S.R.; Bill and Joe Ryan at Atlas Asia-Pacific in San Mateo, California; Frank J. Andonoplas at The Northern Trust Bank in Chicago; Julio Kaplan, Pancho Nudelman, and Juan Salatin at Fric-Rot in Argentina; Stan Zychlinsky and Salvador Rosales at Gabriel de México; Frau Rivers and Herr Lenz, my German teachers, and Señora Black, my Spanish teacher; Ludo Fornasari at Gabriel Europe; Gil Latz of Portland State University and Oregon's International Trade Institute for confirming my Japanese culture lessons a bit; Irving Woolf, sales promotion expert; Samir Sawabini and Nazih Zuraiki in Kuwait; and Joshua Laks in Israel. In gratitude to all of you and the hundreds of people I've met all over the world: peace, good health, good wishes, and thank you!

H.H.R.

# INDEX

## D

## M



## N



## O



## P

## T



## U



## V–W



## X–Z